Napier – An Art Deco City

This publication is a perpetual monthly calendar notebook – so it is not specific to any year and does not expire. This means it does not list the days of the week.

For each month shown this calendar notebook contains:

- A pictorial example of Napier's beautiful art deco buildings

- Important events in Napier's history

- Interesting historical facts and pictures

- Space for you to write in birthdays, anniversaries, or other events

<u>Author:</u>
J.D. McCardle

<u>Published by:</u>
Capital Strategy
PO Box 60029
Auckland 0642
New Zealand

ISBN: 978-0-473-41706-2

Disclaimer: Whilst reasonable care has been taken to prepare this document, no responsibility or liability is accepted for any errors or omissions in the information provided.

The Early History and the Origins of Napier

Napier (Ahuriri in Maori), on the East Coast of New Zealand, is a popular destination for tourists and is one of the prime stops for cruise ships. The Māori name for Napier, Ahuriri, comes from the Māori chief Tu Ahuriri. The Māori name for Hawke Bay is Te Matau-a-Māui from the legend of the fish-hook with which Maui fished up the North Island.

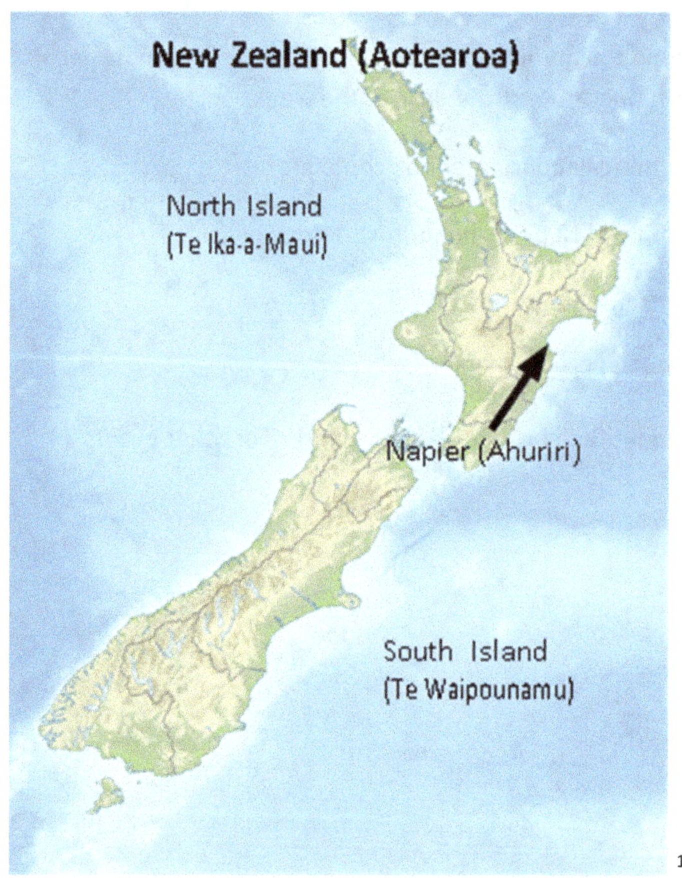

Maori originally settled in Hawke's Bay in the period between 1250-1300AD. The people who became Ngati Kahungunu, the predominant iwi in the region, arrived in the Hawkes's Bay during the 16th century. The waka, or canoe, that brought the original descendants of the Ngati Kahungunu iwi was called "Takitimu." The name of the commander of the waka was Tamatea Arikinui, and one of his sons was called Kahungunu.

The crew of the waka Takitimu became the ancestors of the Ngati Porou, Ngati Kahungunu, and the Ngai Tahu tribe of the South Island

Following Captain James Cook's voyage in 1769 when Hawke Bay was sighted, no further Europeans visited Hawke's Bay until after 1830. During this period, the first visitors were traders, whalers, and missionaries. The first European settlers arrived in the region in the early 1850s.

---

[1] Source: "New Zealand relief map" NordNordWest derivative work: Виктор В, Wikimedia Commons (CC BY-SA) / annotated from original.

The Crown purchased the Ahuriri block (including the site of Napier) in 1851.

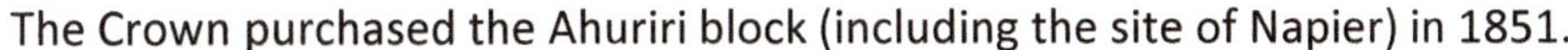

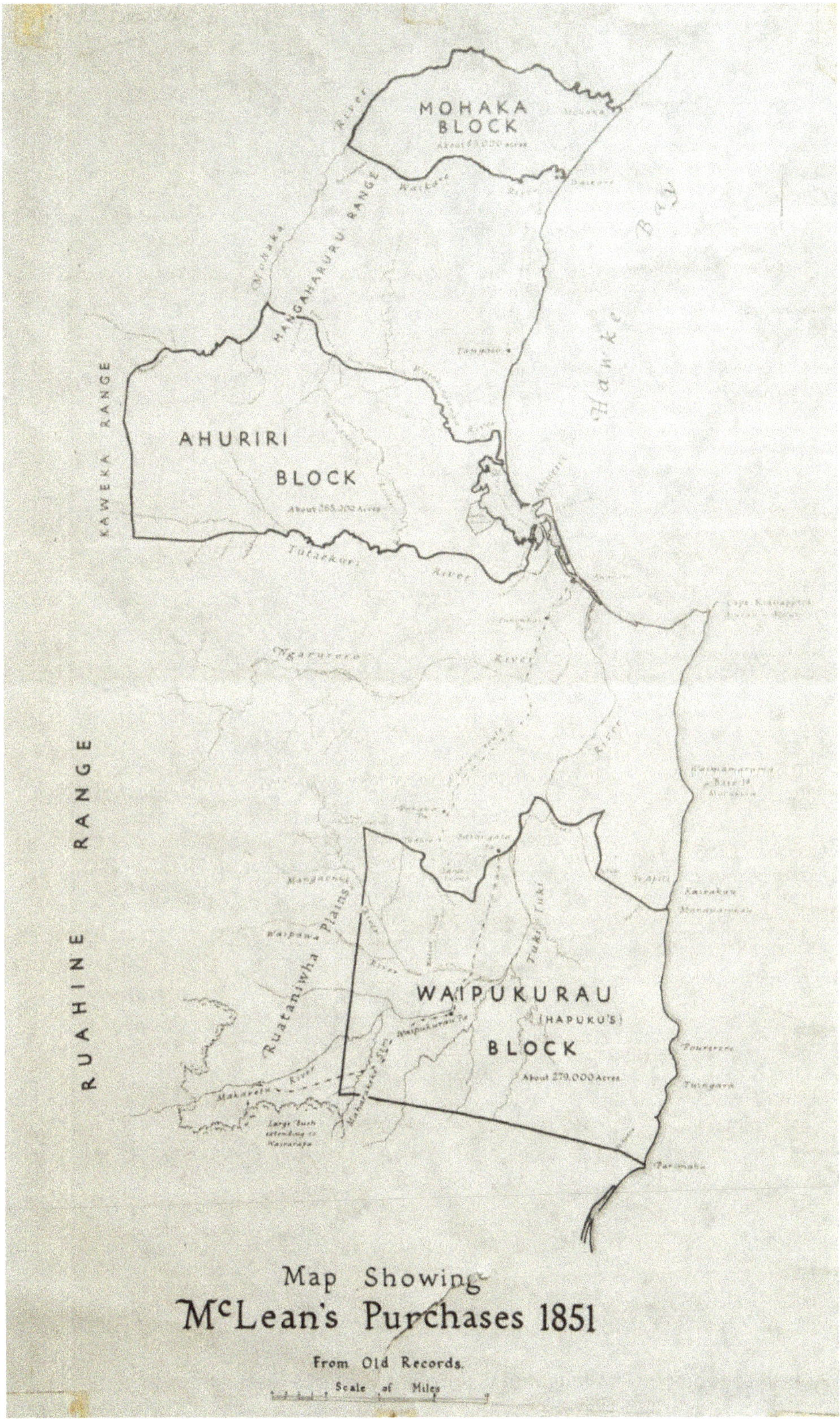

Map, photocopy, McLean's purchases, 1851.[2]

---

[2] Map, photocopy, McLean's purchases, 1851, gifted by Mrs Pomeroy, collection of Hawke's Bay Museums Trust, Ruawharo Tā-ū-rangi, m99.97.17.

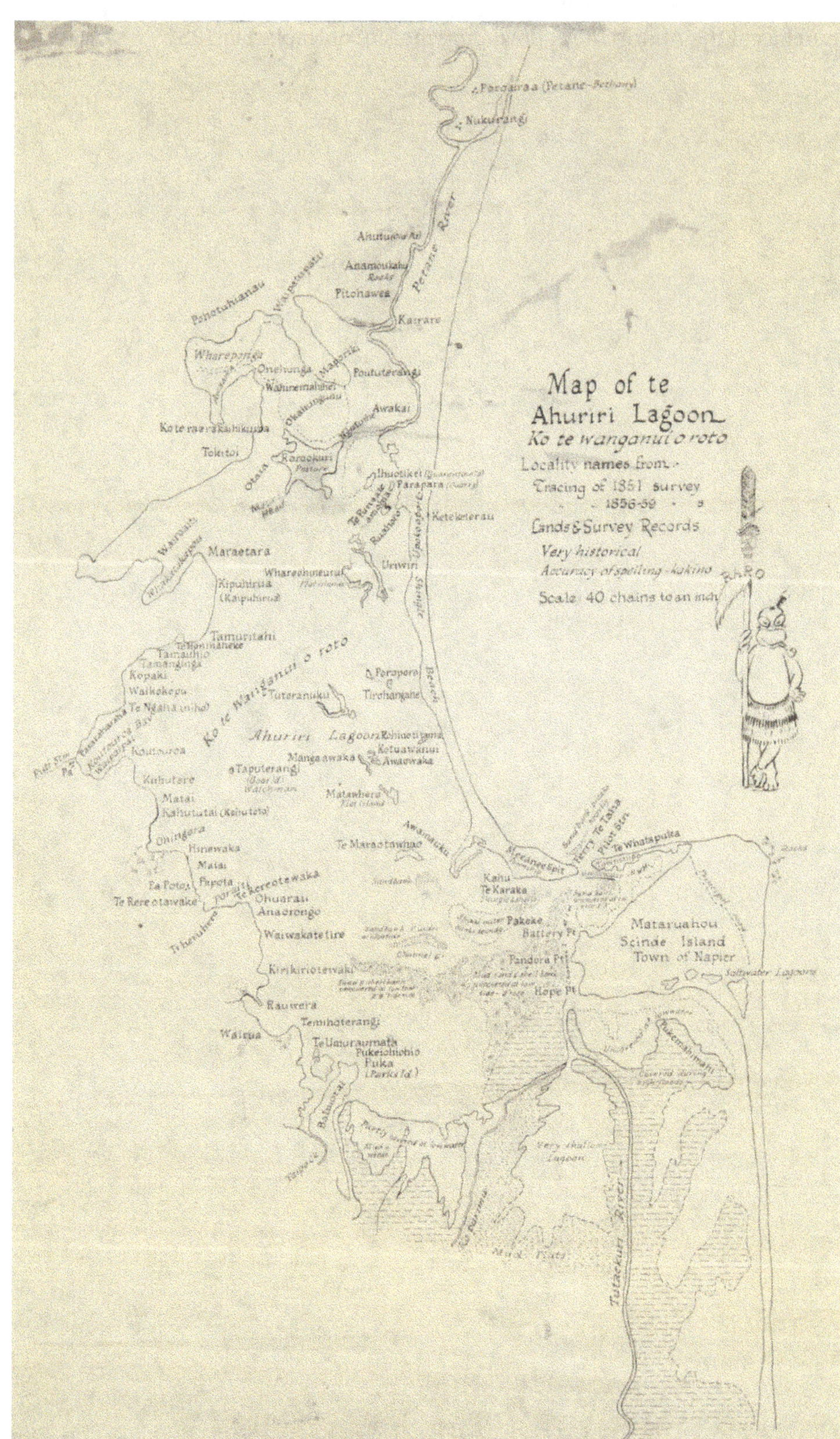

Map of Te Ahuriri Lagoon (Ko Te Wanganui O Roto) and various local names at the time, from a tracing of an 1881 survey and 1856-1859 surveys by the Department of Lands & Survey[3].

---

[3] **Source: Map, Te Ahuriri Lagoon,** collection of Hawke's Bay Museums Trust, Ruawharo Tā-ū-rangi, [71122].

The name Napier was adopted in 1858, and commemorates Sir Charles Napier, the commander-in-chief of British forces in India.

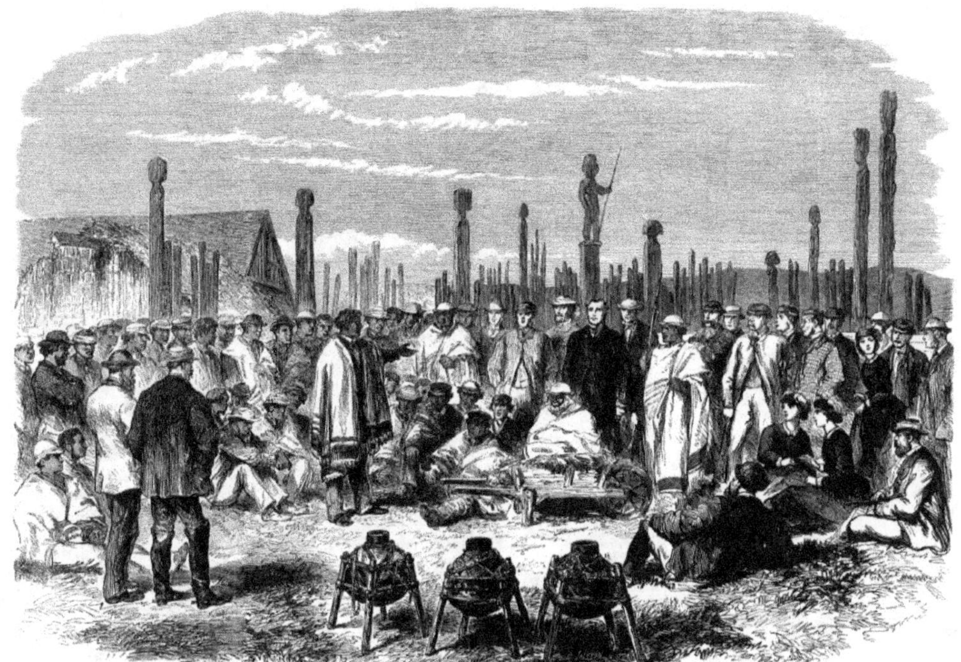

Picture: Engraving from the October 31 1863 Illustrated London News, entitled "Meeting of Settlers and Maoris at Hawke's Bay, New Zealand.[4] "

The engraving, based on photographs taken by Mr. Charles H. Robson, shows the meeting held on the 20th of July 1862 at the Pa[5] Whakairo located about ten miles from Napier near Waiohiki and the Redcliffe bridge. The meeting was to celebrate the completion of a large flour mill erected by the local Maori, with the assistance of the Government.

Mr. Donald McLean, the government's representative and the Superintendent of the then province of Hawke's Bay is near the centre of the engraving (without a hat).

The Maori population at the time was about 3600 and the European population about 2600.

Napier became a borough in 1874 and between 1858 and 1876 Napier was the administrative centre for the province of Hawke's Bay until in 1876 the NZ Parliament dissolved all the provincial governments in New Zealand.

There were significant marshlands and as a result most of the development in the area took place on the hill areas and the port area of Ahuriri.

Napier was rebuilt following a devastating earthquake on the 3rd of February 1931, and as a result has one of the world's best collections of art deco buildings.

---

[4] Restored image by Adam Cuerden. CC BY-SA 3.0

[5] A pā is a Maori village

January

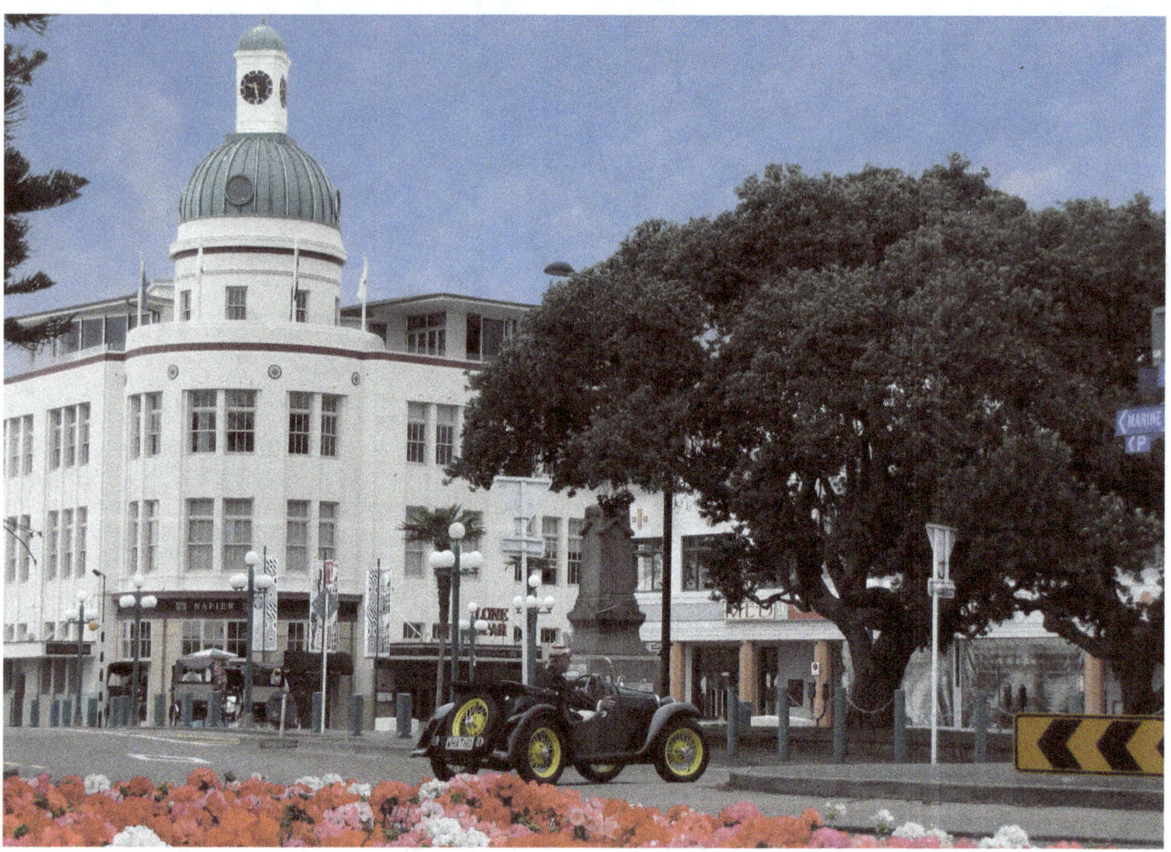

The T&G building at 1 Emerson Street was constructed during the period 1935-36. The architectural firm was Atkin & Mitchell (Wellington) and the builder was WM Angus. Its style is described as Stripped Classical. The original owner was the Australian T&G Mutual Life Insurance Society (where T&G stood for Temperance & General). The company, which was one of the largest insurance companies in Australasia, built many landmark buildings.

Memorable events in January:

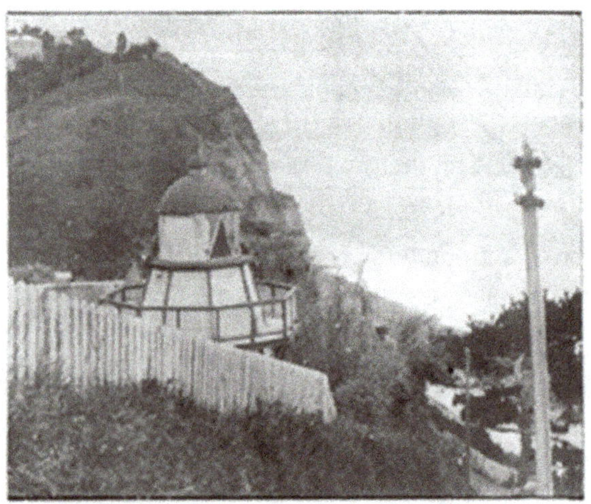

The light of the Napier lighthouse, located at the jail in Coote Road on Bluff Hill, was first lit on 5 January 1873. The light was powered by the town gas supply and was the first in NZ to do so. The first lighthouse keepers were the prison wardens.

---

[6] "Napier Lighthouse" by Cyclopedia Ltd, The New Zealand Electronic Text Collection (CC BY-SA).

Access to potable water was one of the infrastructure constraints on the growth and development of Napier. In January 1875, the first borough engineer Mr C.E. Peppercorne submitted a scheme for supplying the whole of the town between the swamp, the sea and the hills by means of a well sunk in Raffles Street at a cost of £5,000. A new plant was ordered from England at a cost of £10,000 and by the end of 1877 the new water supply began operating. It included a reservoir in Sealy road which was partly to supply Shakespeare, Cameron and Coote roads and partly to provide a reserve for fire-fighting. [7]

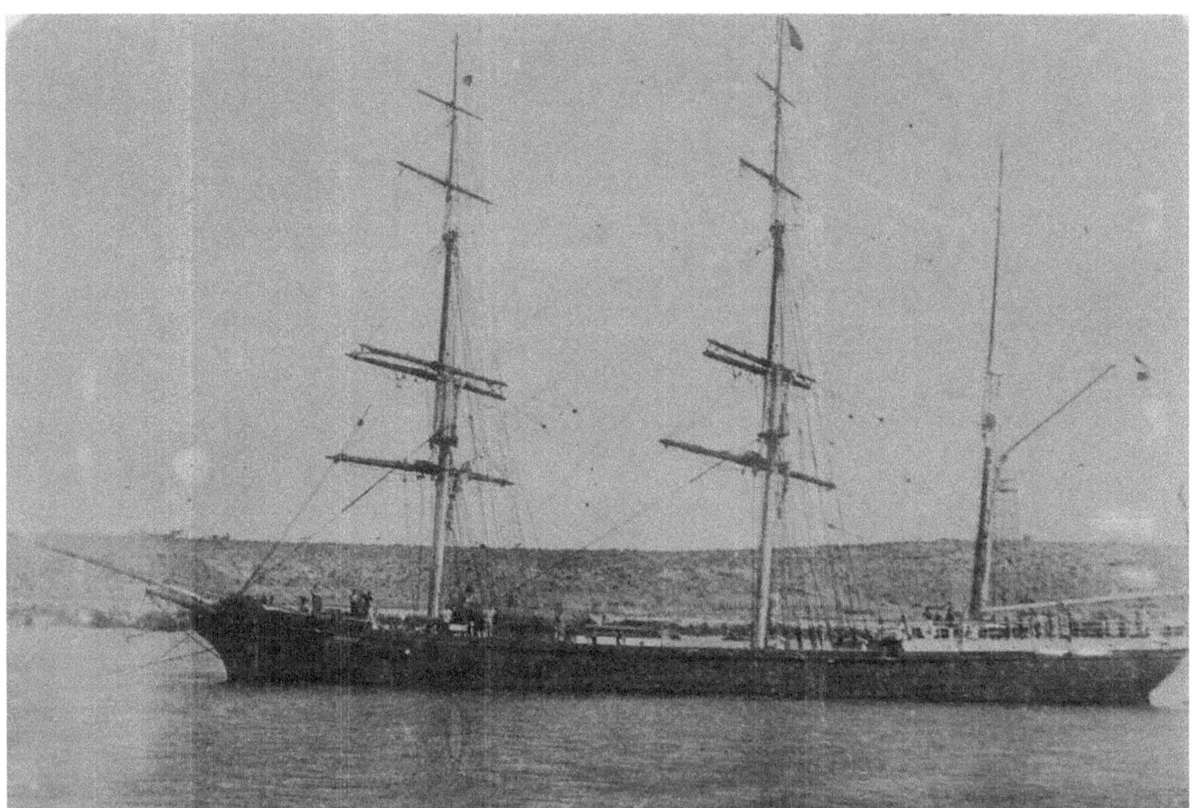

In the month of January 1879, the "barque Adamant" [8] arrived in Napier with 270 immigrants and 23.9 tonnes of cargo on board. It had departed from London on 20 September 1878 sailing via Plymouth. It left Plymouth on 28 September and arrived at Napier on 11 January 1879, having taken 113 days.

On arrival, the immigrants presented the ship's Captain Bowling with the following written thanks signed by all the passengers:

> *"We, the passengers of the ship ADAMANT, cannot suffer to pass unnoticed the very efficient and satisfactory manner by which the captain (T. BOWLING), Mr DALZIEL, the officers and crew, have displayed their duty in conducting the passage from England to New Zealand. Captain BOWLING especially holds the respect and best wishes of all who have been placed under his care."* (Source Hawke's Bay Herald)

---

[7] As reported in the *Jubilee* in 1924

[8] Brodie Collection, La Trobe Picture Collection, State Library of Victoria

The "Adamant " was an iron barque of 3 masts of 739 tonnes, length 53.3 metres, beam 9.1 metres, and depth 5.85 metres. It was built at Hull in 1858. The Adamant made nine voyages to New Zealand under the ownership of the Shaw Savill Company, with its first voyage to Lyttelton in 1873.

The population of the Province of Hawke's Bay from the latest census (and quoting from the census wording itself *"exclusive of aboriginal Natives"*) on the night of the 1st of March 1874 was 9218. With the influx of settlers, by January 1875 Napier had grown to a population of approximately 3514 (presumably of Europeans only, based on the then census recording method) and the town had spread across much of the available land as can be seen in the following engraving. [9]

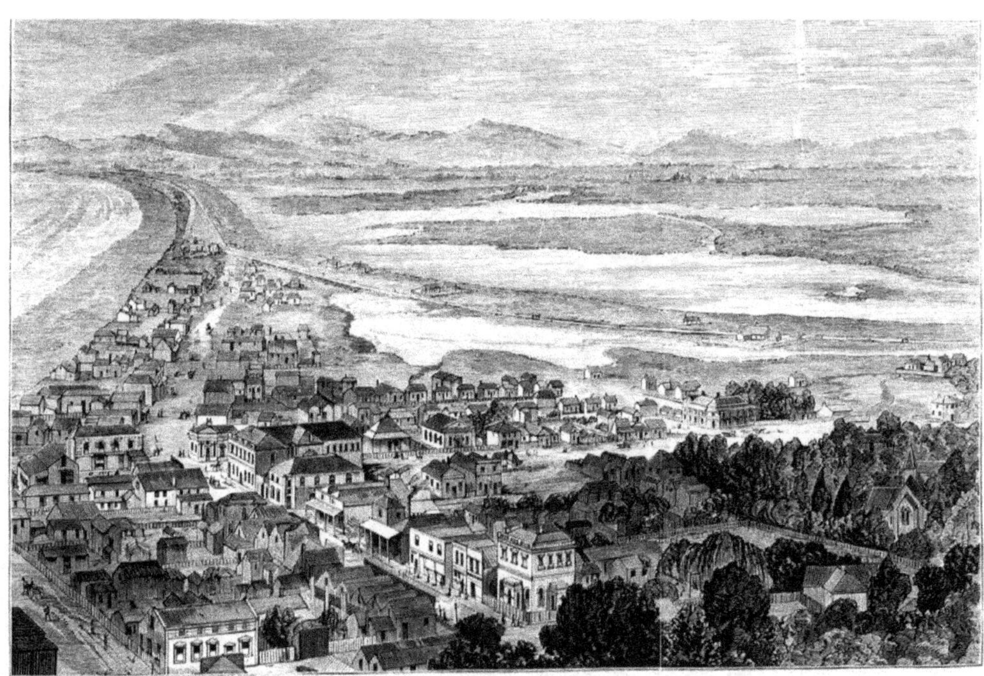

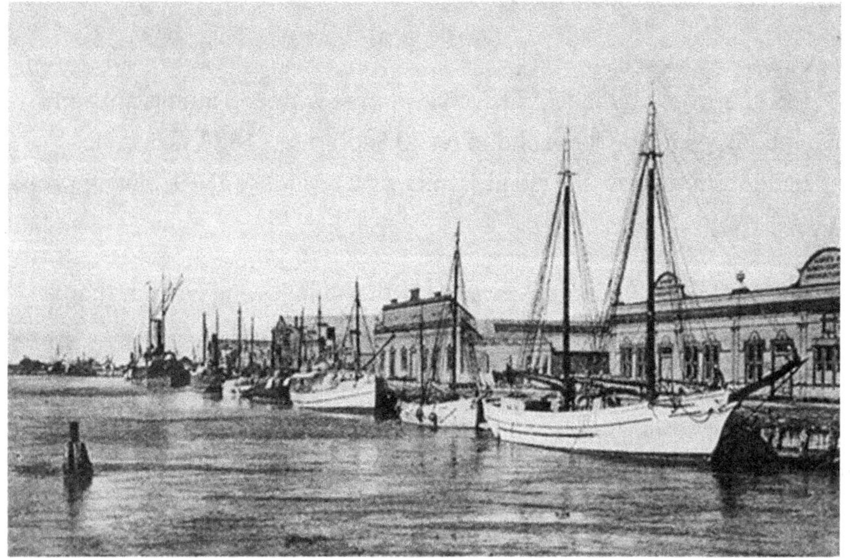

It was a busy time in January as ships arrived in Napier to load up the wool clip for export. This photo from January 2010 shows coastal steamers lining up to load wool to then load on to ships for export to London. [10]

---

[9] Wood engraving of Napier published in the Illustrated Australian News for home readers, January 27, 1875, publisher Ebenezer and David Syme. Source State Library of Victoria.

[10] No known Copyright. From Sir George Grey Special Collections, Auckland Libraries, AWNS-19100120-2-1. Taken from the supplement to the Auckland Weekly News 20 January 1910

In January 1933, almost two years after the earthquake, Napier was declared officially 'reborn' during the New Napier Carnival. This is a poster produced by the NZ Railways publicity branch for the 1933 Napier Carnival:

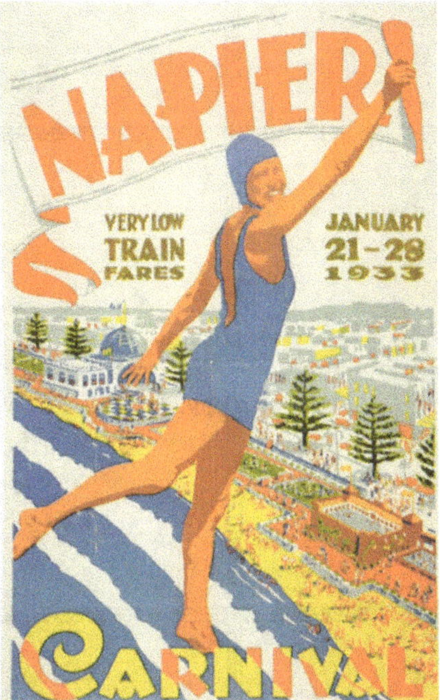

[11]

On the 6th & 7th of January 1954 there was a Royal Tour visit to Hawke's Bay. The Queen and the Duke of Edinburgh were greeted in Napier with a two-mile long avenue of flowers, and a visit to McLean Park, where the highlight was a display of shearing by Ivan and Godfrey Bowen.

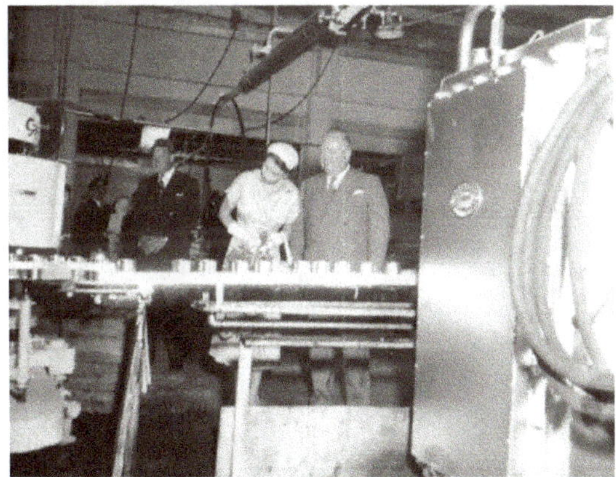

The Queen also visited a range of other places, and these photos[12] show her arriving at Hillview orchard and with Sir James Wattie at the Wattie canneries in Hastings.

The idea of a Napier-based tramping group (the Napier Tramping Club) was born on a tramp at Lake Waikaremoana in January 1974. On October 5, 1974, the club held its inaugural tramp. This was a climb to the summit of the Kaweka Ranges (Kaweka J at 1724 metres is the highest point in Hawke's Bay).

---

[11] "New Zealand Railway Poster" by Archives New Zealand, FLICKR (CC BY-SA).

[12] Photos used with permission by Knowledge Bank - HB Digital Archives Trust www.knowledgebank.org.nz

1	2	3	4
5	6	7	8
9	10	11	12
13	14	15	16
17	18	19	20
21	22	23	24
25	26	27	28
29	30	31	

February

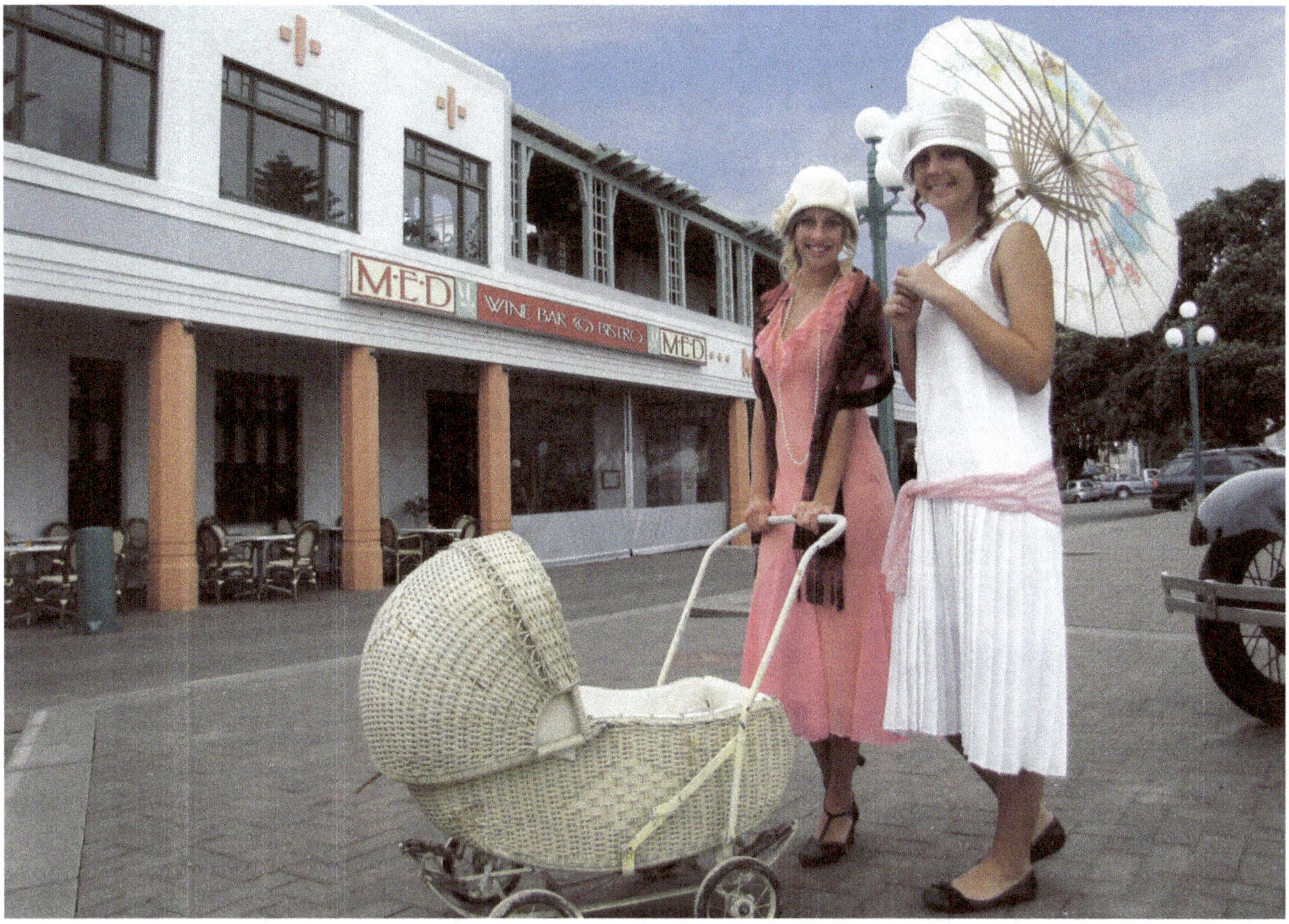

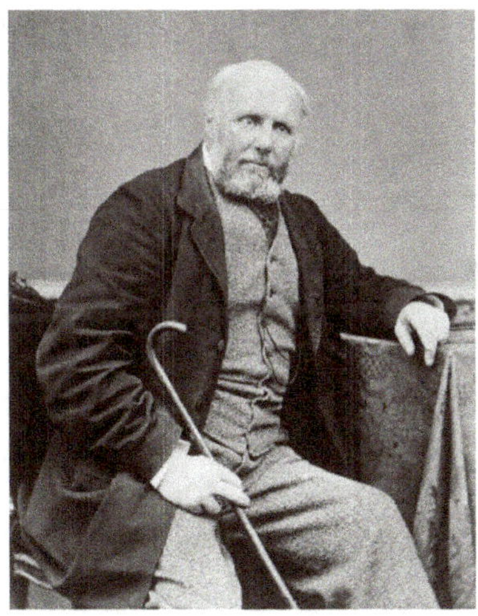

Memorable events in February:

In February 1854 Alfred Domett (Commissioner of Crown Lands and magistrate for Ahuriri) requested that the port town be named after Sir Charles Napier, and he also laid out the first town plan of Napier. The name Napier was adopted in 1858.

Alfred Dommett - c 1870-1887[13]

---

13 National Library NZ on The Commons, Wellington (commons.wikimedia.org/w/index.php?curid=10393893)

In the month of February in 1858 the first overseas wool ship called at Napier (the Southern Cross).

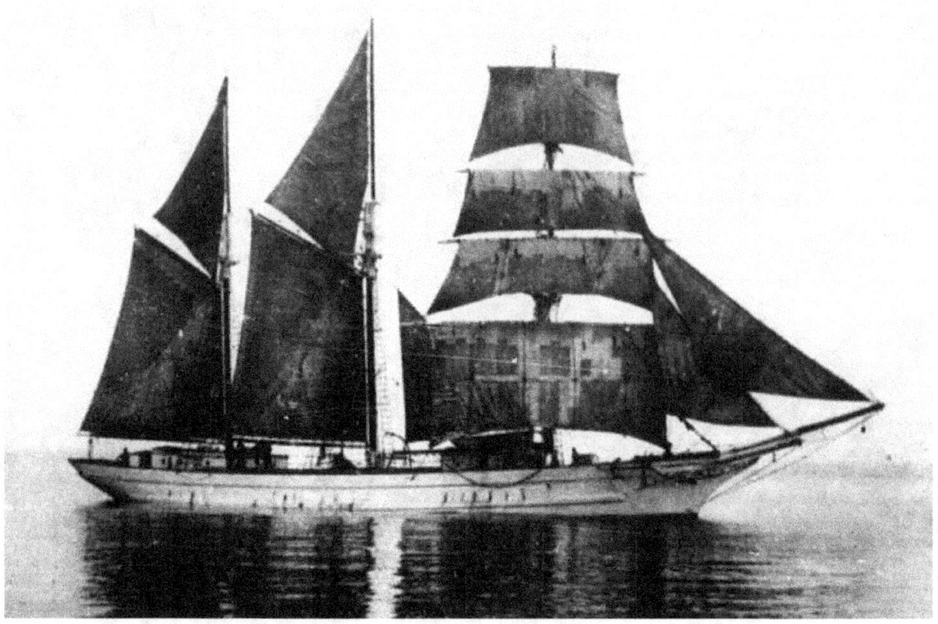

A similar schooner, Southern Cross 4 [14]

On 19 February 1861 Mr. Henry Powning Stark won the first election to the Napier electorate. Henry Powning Stark was an insurance agent in Napier, as well as a freemason and a founder of the Napier Club in 1860. He resigned his seat in the House of Representatives in June 1861 as a consequence of a public debate concerning the obligation of the province of Hawke to meet its share of the debts accrued when it was part of the Wellington province. Following Stark's resignation William Colenso took his seat in a by-election. Stark then became an Auckland land agent and a sharebroker.

The Daily Telegraph newspaper was founded in February 1871 by its first editor, and previous London journalist, Richard Halkett Lord.

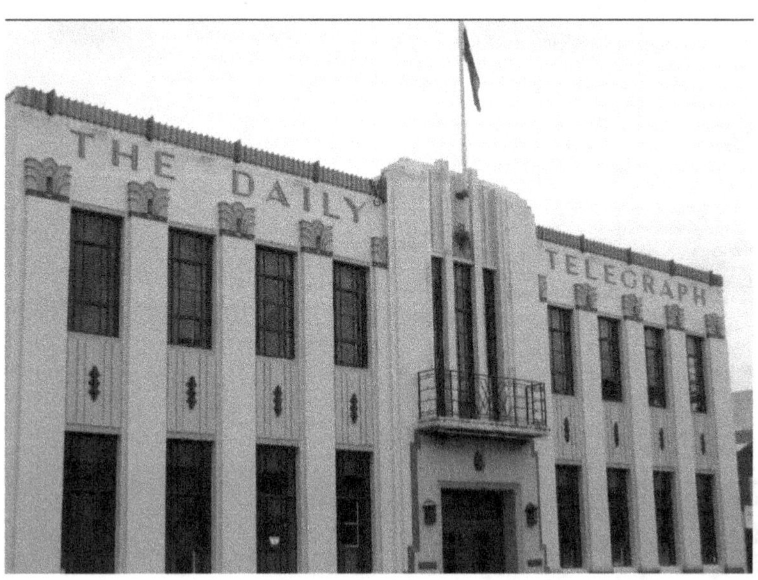

The Daily Telegraph building in Tennyson Street was completed in 1933. It was designed by the architect EA Williams of Napier and built by Fletcher Construction. Its style is described as Art Deco.

---

[14] Item is held by John Oxley Library, the State Library of Queensland. Public Domain (commons.wikimedia.org/w/index.php?curid=14441544)

On 4 February 1875, the first Napier Council meeting was held. Nine councillors were elected at the first election, and Mr Robert Stuart was selected as the first mayor.

At 10.46am on 3 February 1931 Napier, and the surrounding region, was struck by an earthquake measuring 7.8 on the Richter scale. While the ground shook violently for less than three minutes, 256 lives were lost and the majority of buildings in Napier and many in Hastings were destroyed.

The ground at Ahuriri was lifted significantly by the earthquake, by as much as 2.7 metres, turning what was previously sea into new land. The area affected was large; the ground that domed upwards above the fault line was about 90 kilometres long by 15 kilometres wide.

NEW ZEALAND POST OFFICE TELEGRAPHS.

63A.

EASTERN EXTENSION A. & C. TELEGRAPH CO. LTD.   INWARD CABLE MESSAGE: "Via EASTERN"

	Tube No.	Sent at	Govt. Date Stamp.	Eastern Co. Date Stamp.
(time)	46	To	−4 FEB 1931	4 FEB
Initials		By		4 27 AM WN
	Checked by	Ack. recd. by		

VIA EASTERN

XNZ   22   LONDONPO   59   3RD   2 30PM
ETAT

THE GOVERNOR GENERAL WELLINGTON   NZ

THE QUEEN AND I ARE MUCH CONCERNED TO HEAR
OF THE EARTHQUAKE IN THE NORTH ISLAND
INVOLVING LOSS OF LIFE AND DAMAGE TO PROPERTY
PLEASE CONVEY OUR SYMPATHY TO THOSE WHOSE
RELATIVES AND FRIENDS HAVE PERISHED AND WHOSE
HOMES HAVE BEEN WRECKED I SHOULD LIKE
   FURTHER INFORMATION ESPECIALLY REGARDING THE
INJURED
      GEORGE R I

Telegraph from the King and Queen[15]

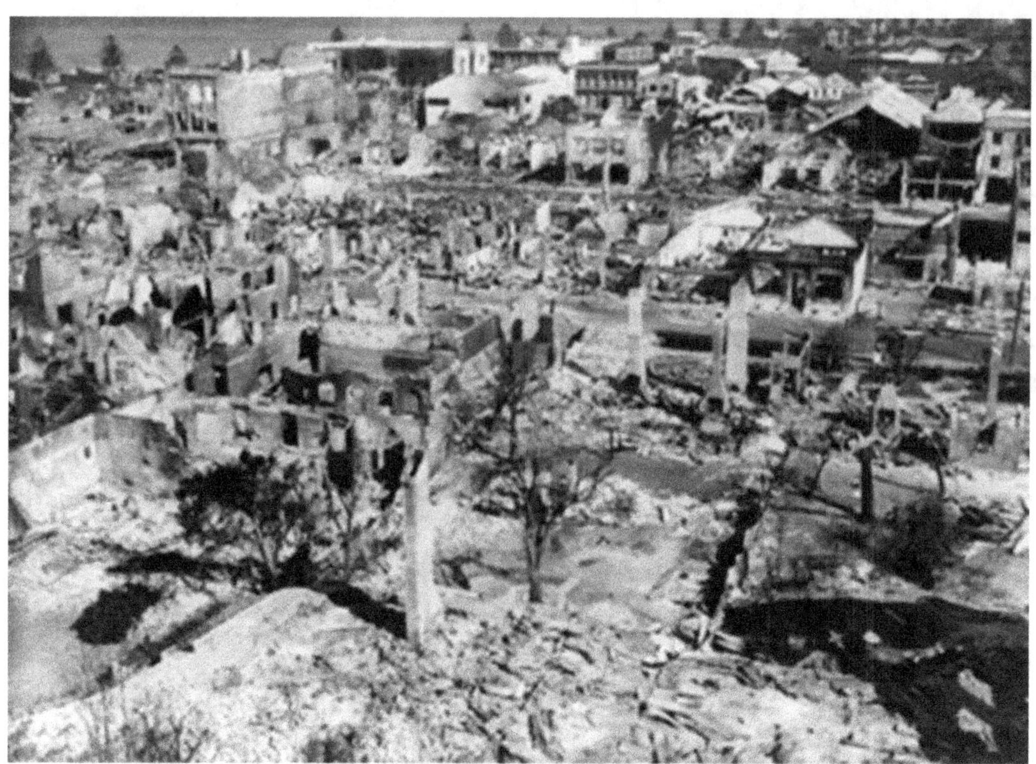

Ruins of downtown Napier after the earthquake [16]

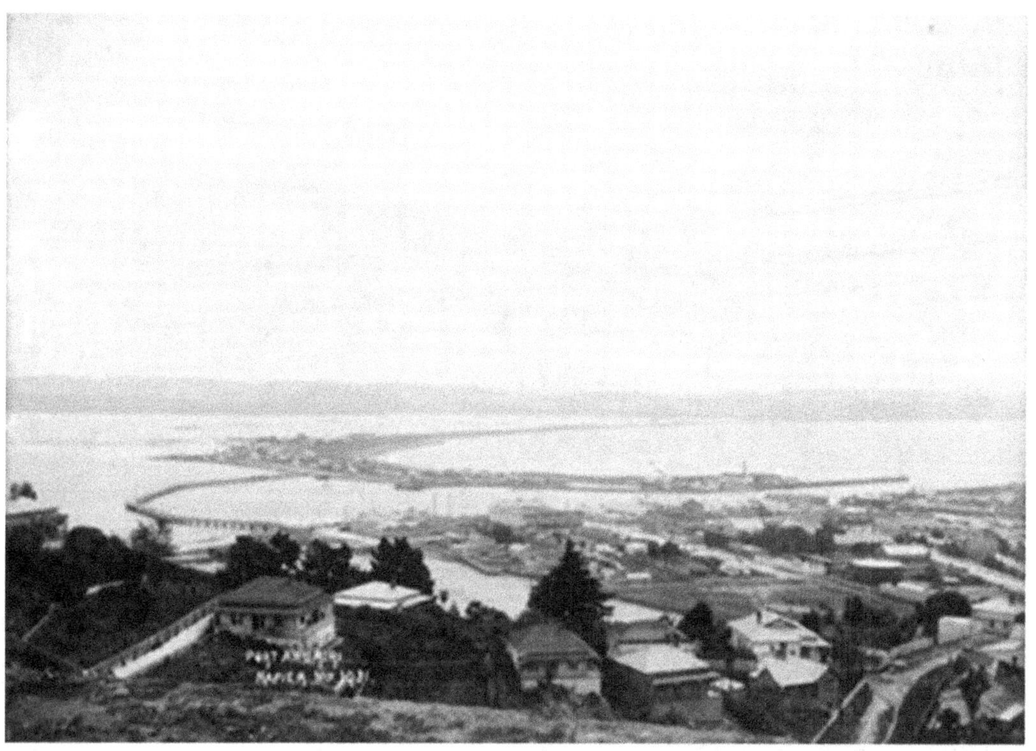

Port Ahuriri before the earthquake [17]

[16] We acknowledge the New Zealand GeoNet project & its sponsors EQC, GNS Science & LINZ, for providing these images
[17] Ibid

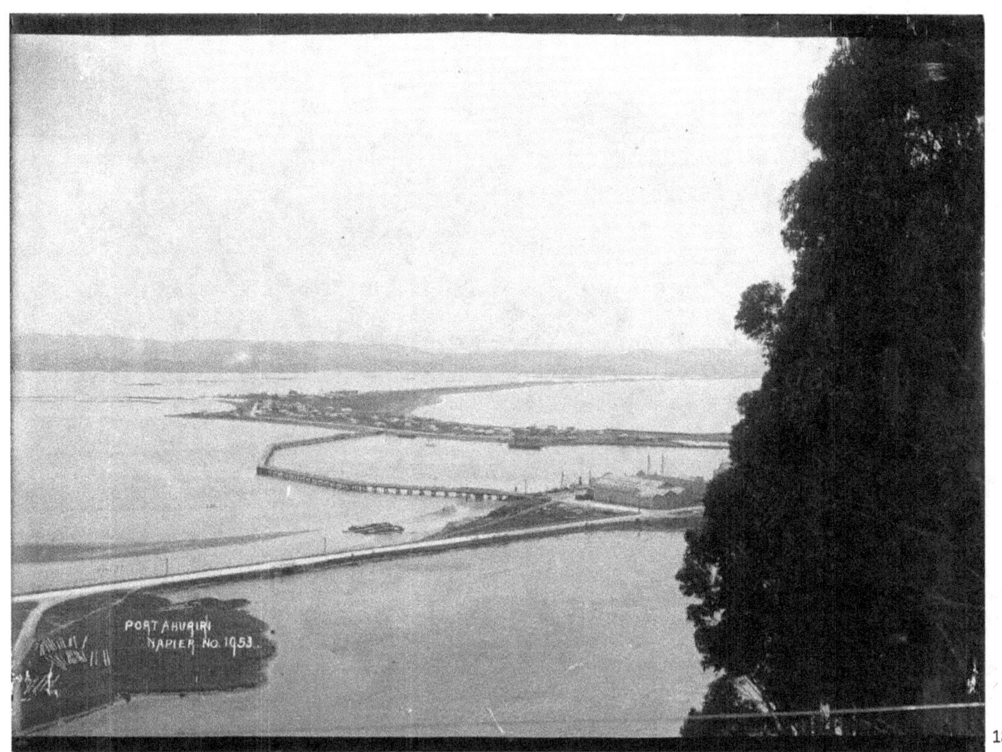

Another view of Port Ahuriri before the earthquake

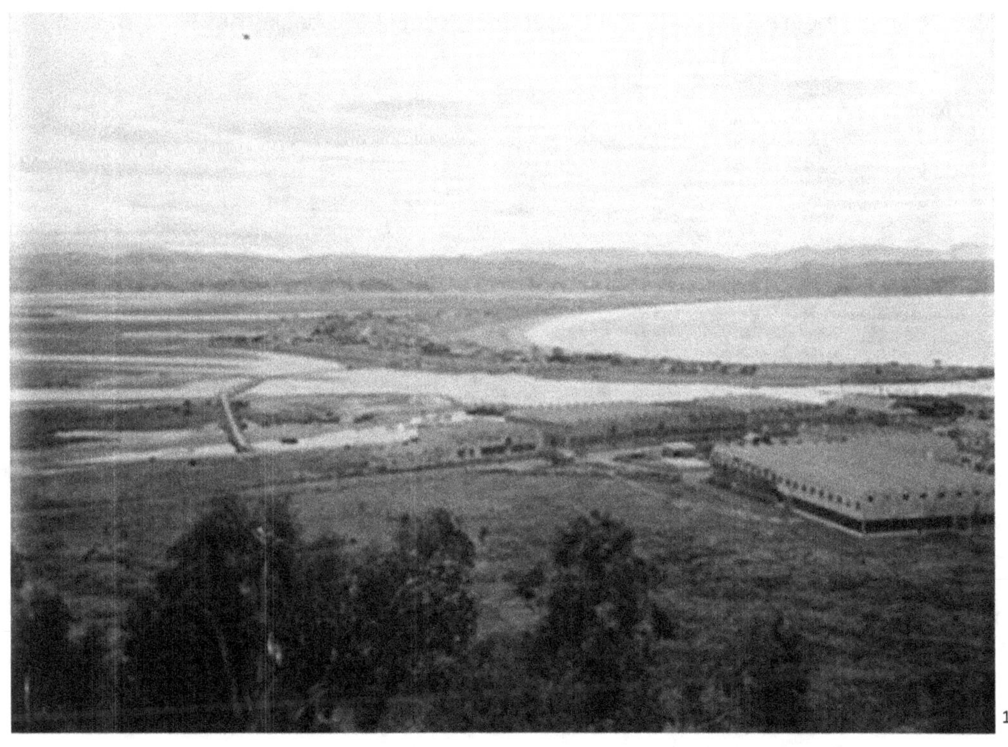

Ahuriri after the earthquake showing lifting of the ground

[18] Port Ahuriri, Napier. Price, William Archer, 1866-1948: Collection of post card negatives. Ref: 1/2-001382-G. Alexander Turnbull Library, Wellington, New Zealand. /records/22756033

[19] We acknowledge the New Zealand GeoNet project & its sponsors EQC, GNS Science & LINZ, for providing these images

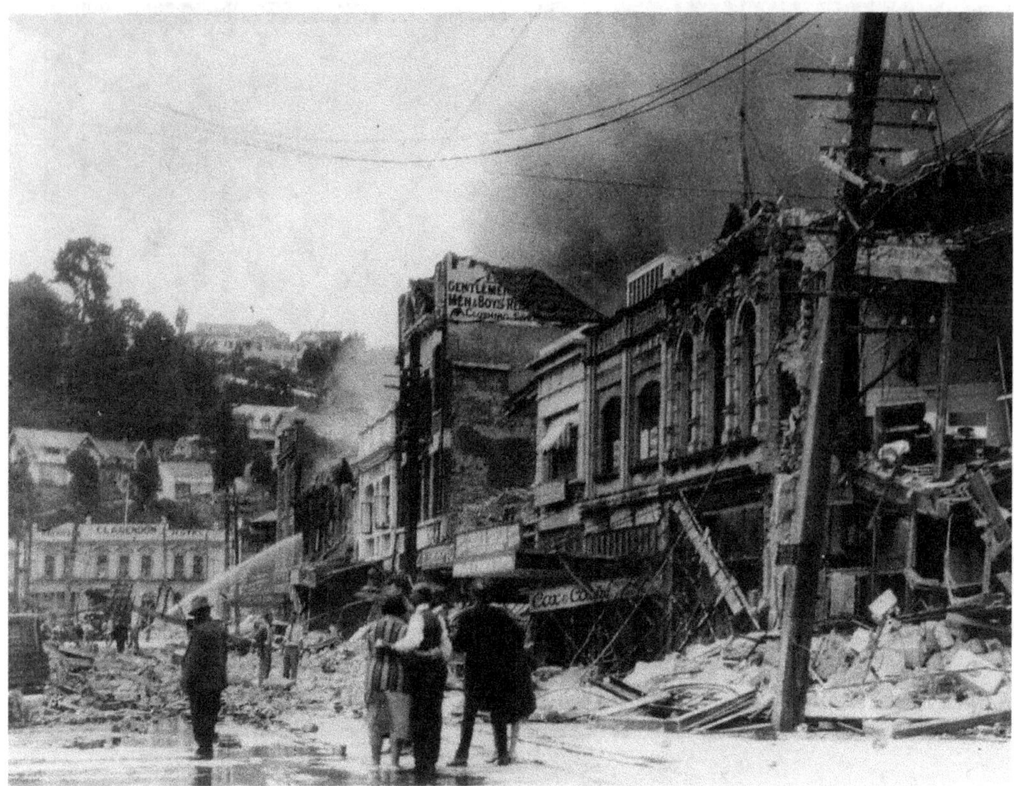

Shakespeare Road with the Clarendon Hotel in the background

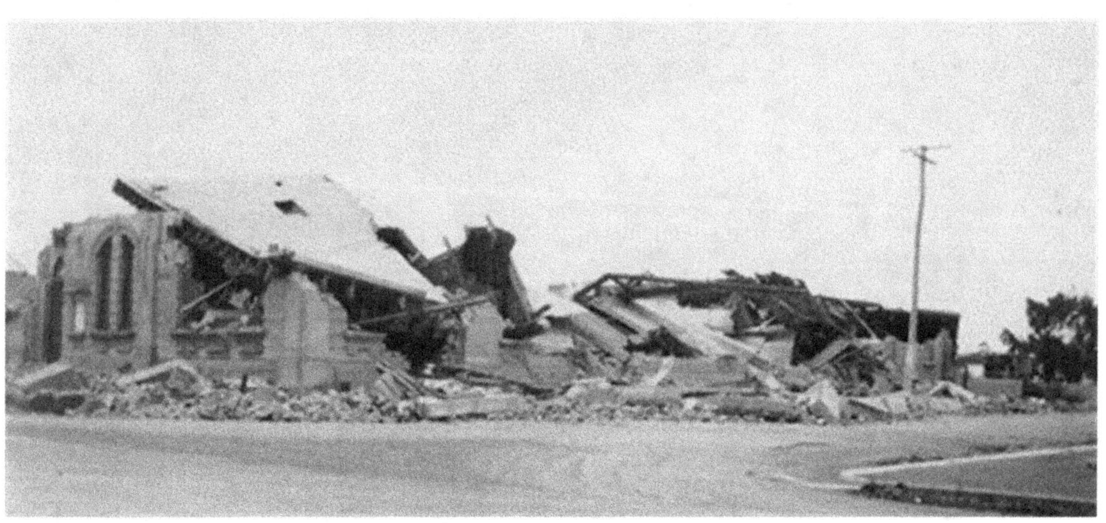

Taradale Town Hall after the 1931 earthquake [21]

[20] Archives NZ (CC by 2.0)

[21] "Town Hall, Taradale," John Brown, photographer, gifted by Mrs Selina Brown, collection of Hawke's Bay Museums Trust, Ruawharo Tā-ū-rangi, 9126

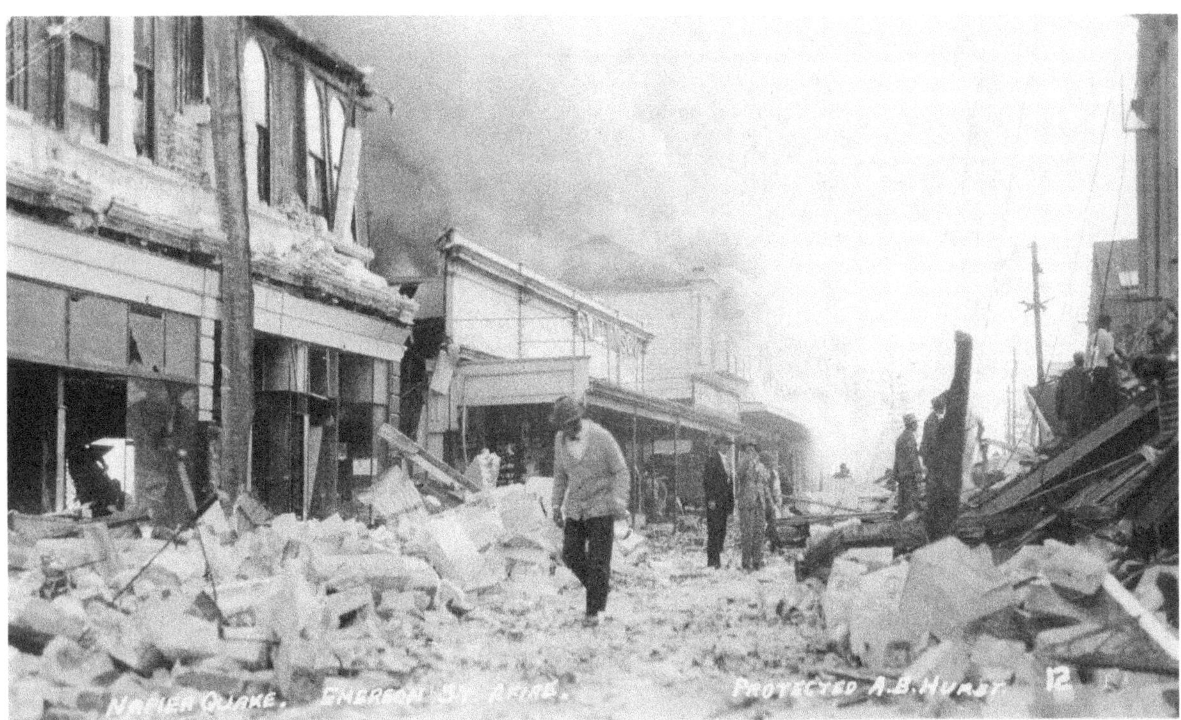

Fire in Emerson Street after the Napier earthquake[22]

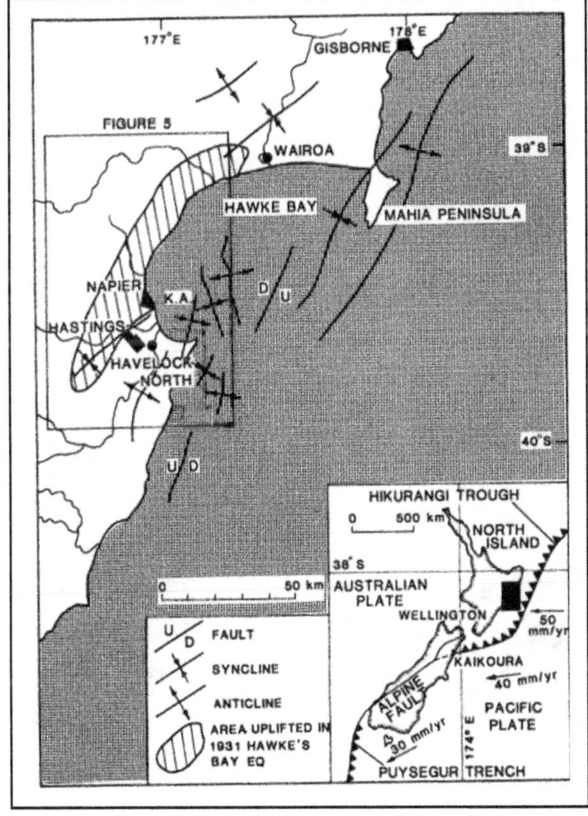

Tectonic setting of the 1931 earthquake [23]

---

[22] Napier Earthquake - Emerson Street afire, circa 1931, Napier, by Arthur Hurst. Gift of Mrs J Paterson, date unknown. Te Papa Collection (O.005480)

[23] Alan G. Hull (1990) Tectonics of the 1931 Hawke's Bay earthquake, New Zealand Journal of Geology and Geophysics, 33:2, 309-320, DOI: 10.1080/00288306.1990.10425689. Page 310.

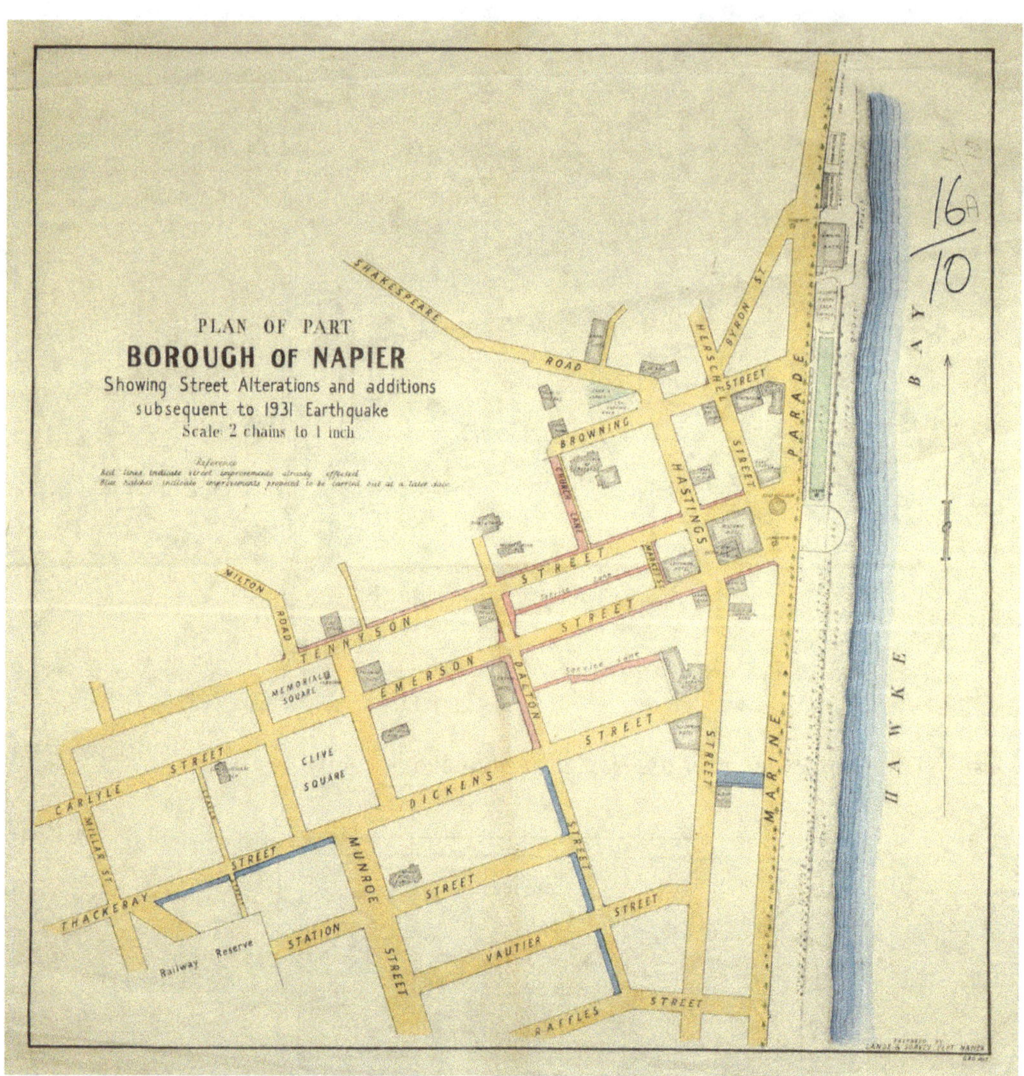

Street plan of part of Napier following the earthquake[24]

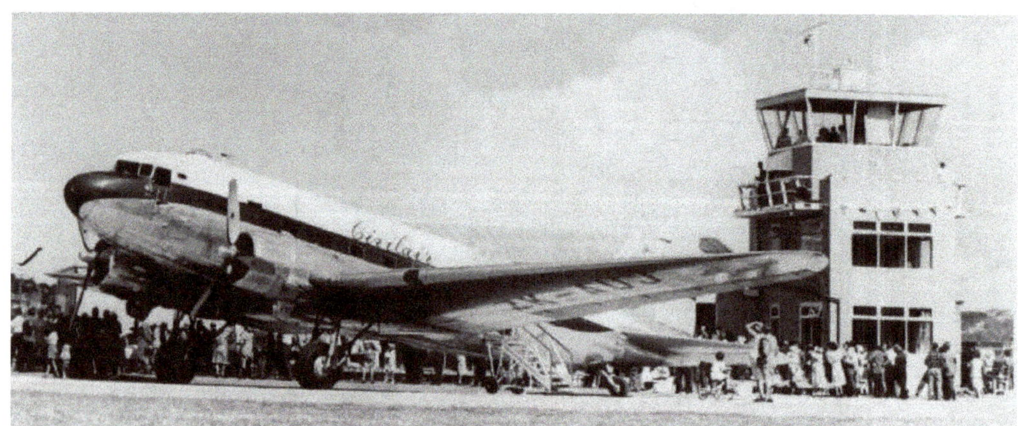

Hawke's Bay Airport on the outskirts of Napier was officially opened on the 15th of February 1964.

---

[24] Archives NZ (CC by 2.0)

[25] Photo used with permission of Hawke's Bay Airport Ltd.

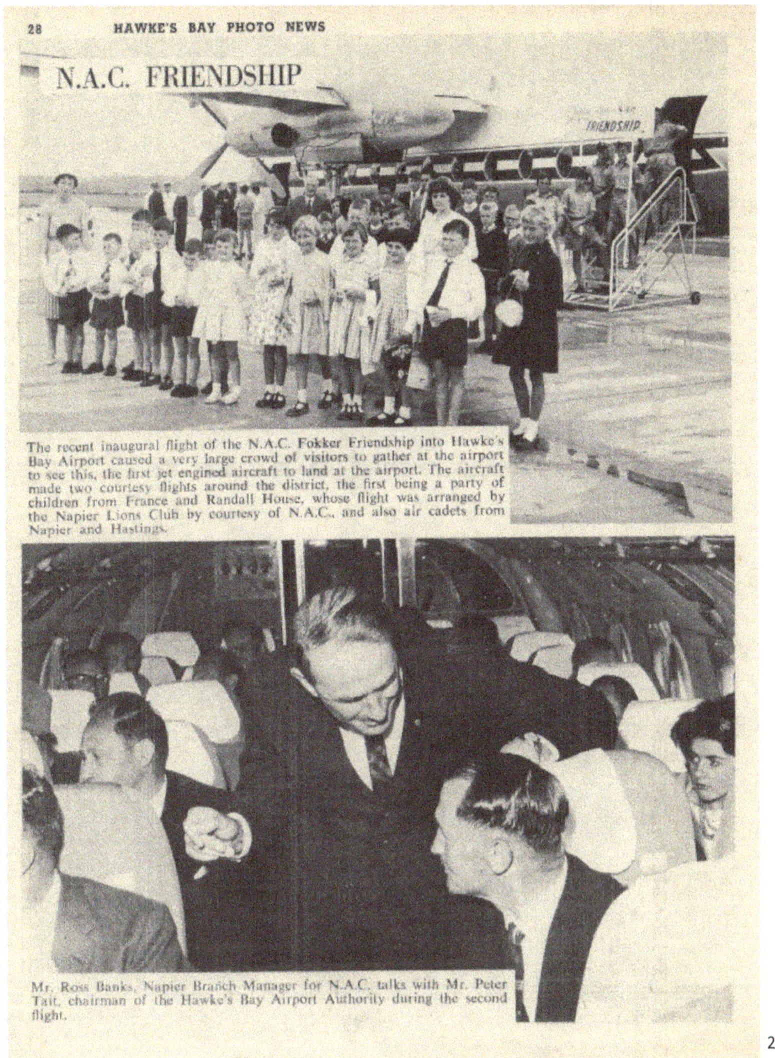

The recent inaugural flight of the N.A.C. Fokker Friendship into Hawke's Bay Airport caused a very large crowd of visitors to gather at the airport to see this, the first jet engined aircraft to land at the airport. The aircraft made two courtesy flights around the district, the first being a party of children from France and Randall House, whose flight was arranged by the Napier Lions Club by courtesy of N.A.C., and also air cadets from Napier and Hastings.

Mr. Ross Banks, Napier Branch Manager for N.A.C. talks with Mr. Peter Tait, chairman of the Hawke's Bay Airport Authority during the second flight.

[26]

There had been flights from the airfield for many years before, with the first regular service between Napier and Gisborne commencing in 1935. This first service was run by East Coast Airways Ltd using a twin-engine De Havilland Dragon DH-84 II aircraft similar to the one in this photo:

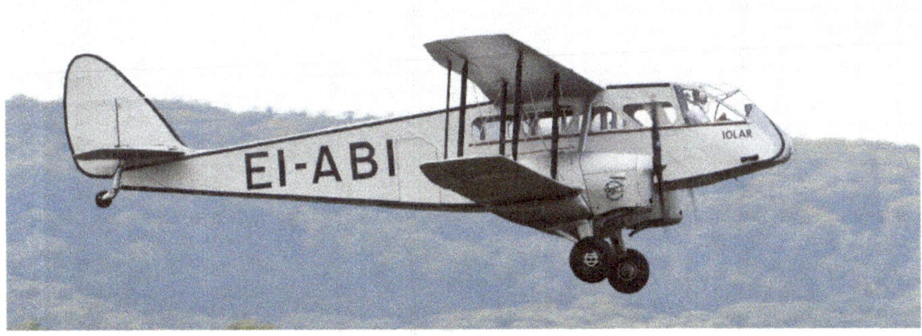

East Coast Airways issued special commemorative first day covers for the occasion.

1	2	3	4
5	6	7	8
9	10	11	12
13	14	15	16
17	18	19	20
21	22	23	24
25	26	27	28

March

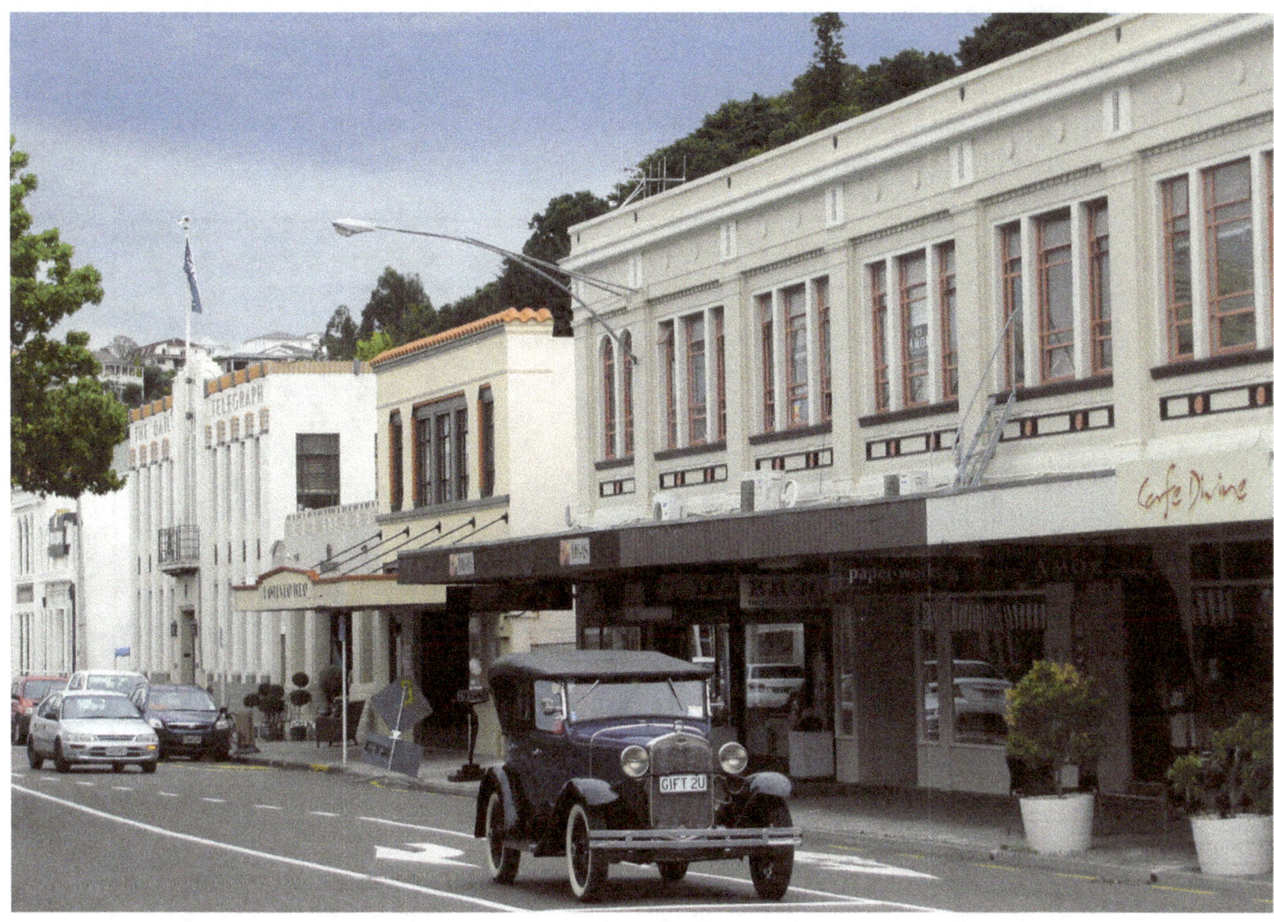

The building in the foreground is the Bryant's building on the corner of Hastings and Tennyson streets. It was designed by the architect Finch & Westerholm of Napier and built by A Bryan, being completed in 1933.

The Bryant building housed a range of retailers and services, including JH Fargher and Company who were clothiers and Outfitters, a dental surgeon SH Hole and HJ Bailey a jeweller.

The second building visible in the above photo is the former McGlashan's Building at 39 Tennyson Street that was completed in 1932. Its architect was Finch & Westerholm of Napier and the builder was AB Davis. Its style is described as Spanish Mission.

It housed an auction mart and offices.

Memorable events in March:

In March 1859 the first church in Napier, the Roman Catholic St Mary's church, was built in Shakespeare Road.

In March 1932, following the 1931 earthquake, nineteen shops in Hastings Street and Tennyson Street were ready for occupation.

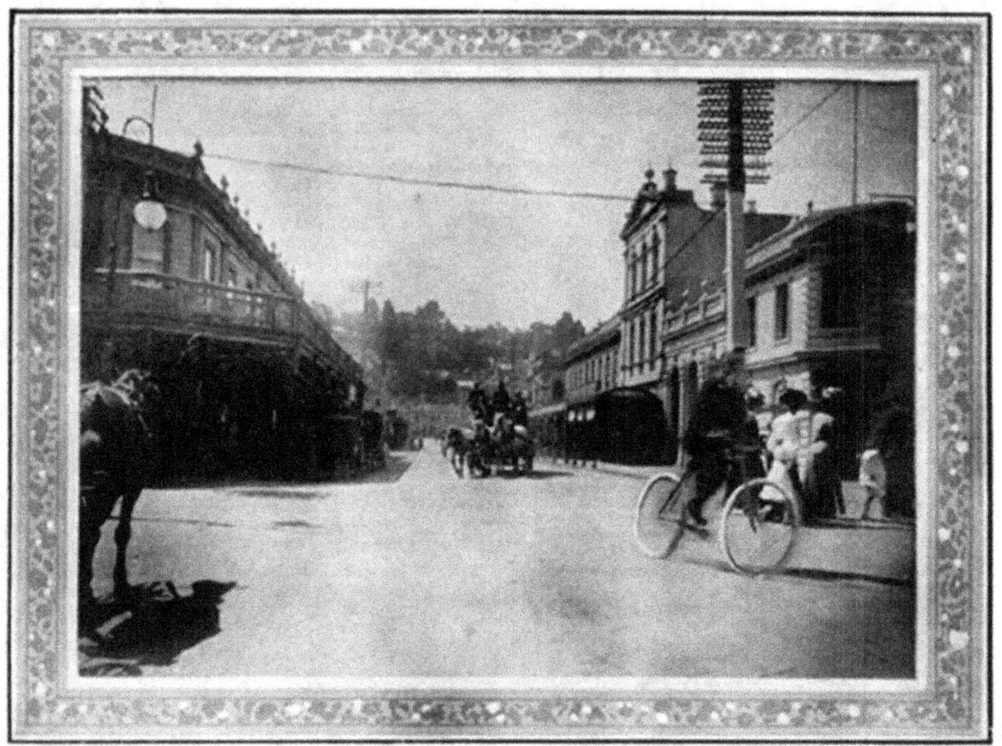

Hastings Street, looking north

In March 1950 Napier became a city when it reached the population of 20,000. The council spent the princely sum of $1342 on the celebrations, as the following excerpt shows, from legislation in 1950 validating the expenditure in the transition to the new body.

Local Legislation Act 1950
Public Act   1950 No 79

13   Validating certain expenditure incurred by Napier City Council in connection with certain celebrations

The expenditure incurred by the Napier City Council during the financial year ended on 31 March 1950 in connection with the celebration of the 75th anniversary of the establishment of the Borough of Napier and also in the celebration of the proclamation of the said borough as a city, amounting to the sum of $1,342.21 and two-thirds cents, and the payment of the said sum by payments amounting to the sum of $651.45 and five-sixths cents during the financial year ended on 31 March 1950, and by payments amounting to the sum of $690.75 and five-sixths cents during the financial year ending on 31 March 1951, are hereby validated and declared to have been lawfully incurred and made.

---

[27] "Hastings Street archive photo" by Cyclopedia Ltd, The New Zealand Electronic Text Collection (CC BY-SA).

In March 1955 a floral clock, which was a gift from Mr and Mrs A.B. Hurst, was installed on a site between the baths and the Tom Parker Fountain.

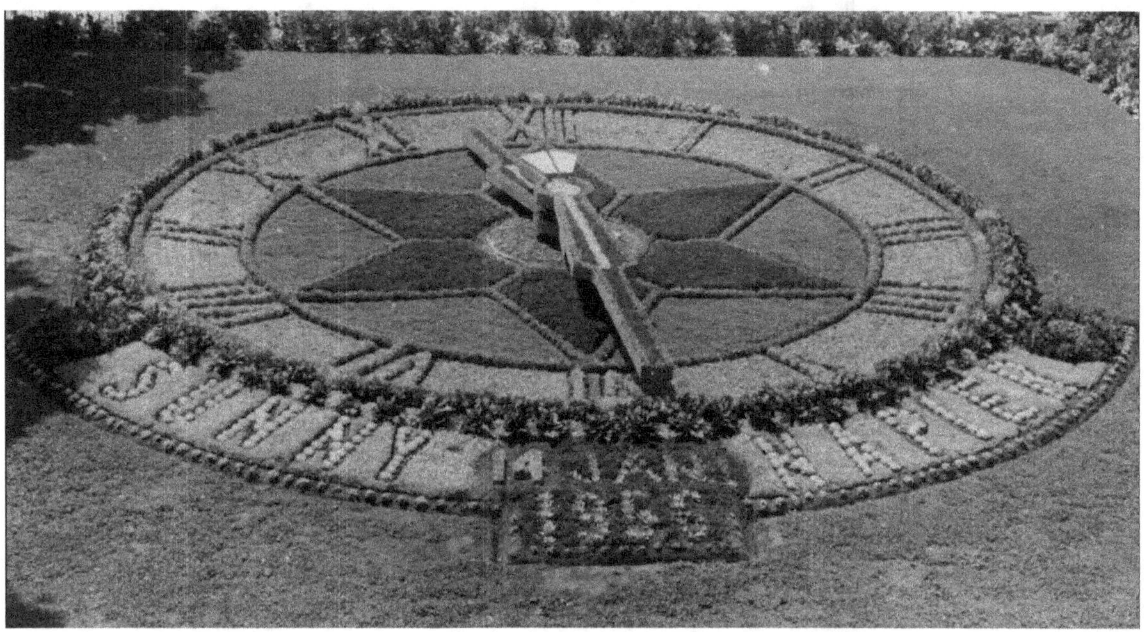

In the month of March in 1965 the new Anglican cathedral was completed.

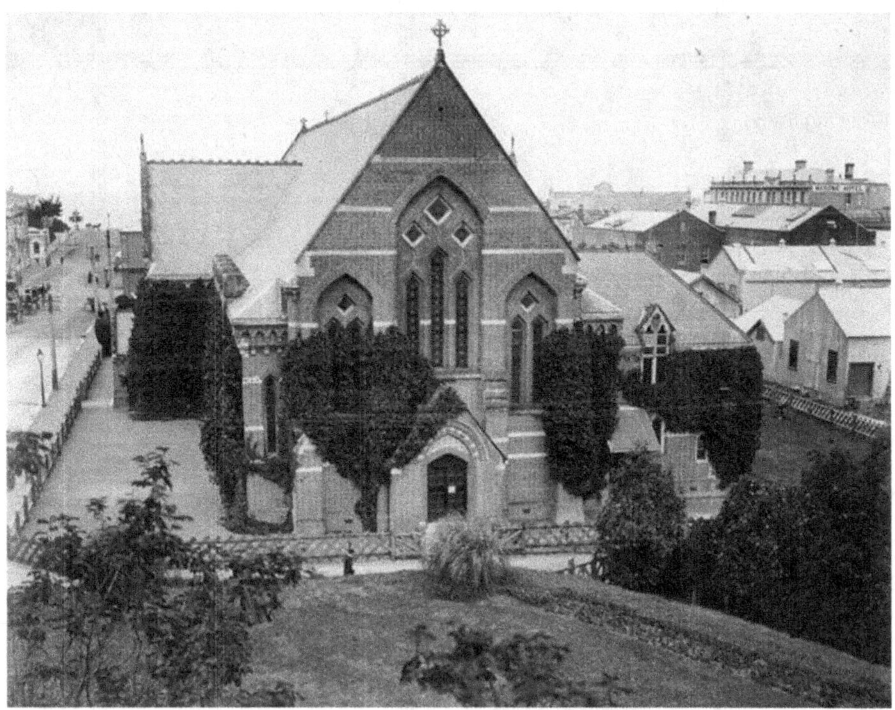

St John's Anglican cathedral, Napier 1907

---

[28] Floral Clock Marine Parade by R Foxley, January 1956. Photo used with permission by Knowledge Bank - HB Digital Archives Trust

[29] "St John's Anglican Cathedral, Napier," gifted by Mrs and Miss Pallot, collection of Hawke's Bay Museums Trust, Ruawharo Tā-ū-rangi, 1804

1	2	3	4
5	6	7	8
9	10	11	12
13	14	15	16
17	18	19	20
21	22	23	24
25	26	27	28
29	30	31	

April

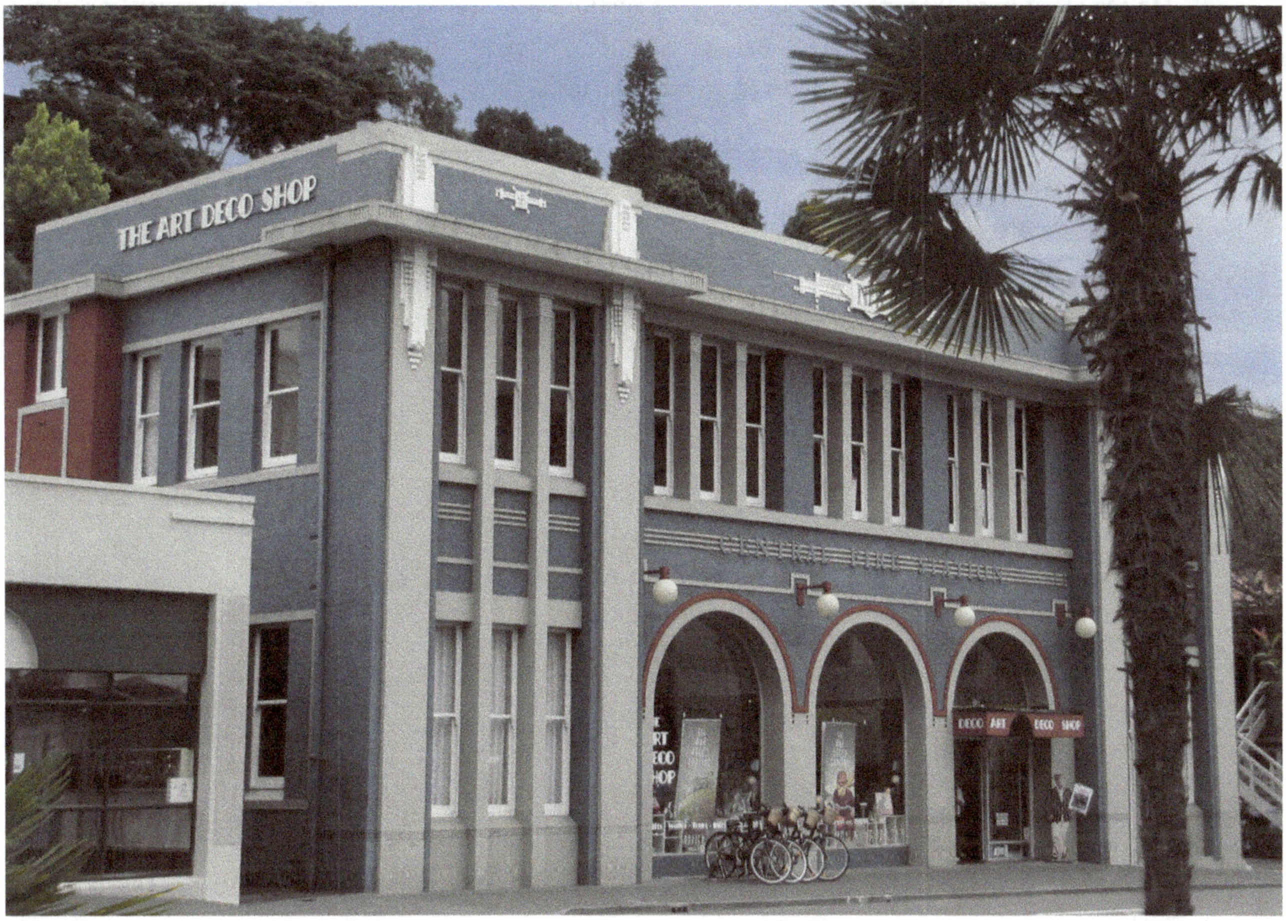

This building was the previous home for the Art Deco Trust and shop and originally was the Napier central fire station. The building was converted to offices in 1969. This photo was taken shortly before the Art Deco Trust relocated. The architect for the building was JA Louis Hay of Napier, and the builder was Trevor Bros Ltd. The date of completion was 1926 and refurbishment was completed in 1932 to the same design (substituting reinforced concrete for the original brick façade) after the earthquake. Its style is described as Prairie Style.

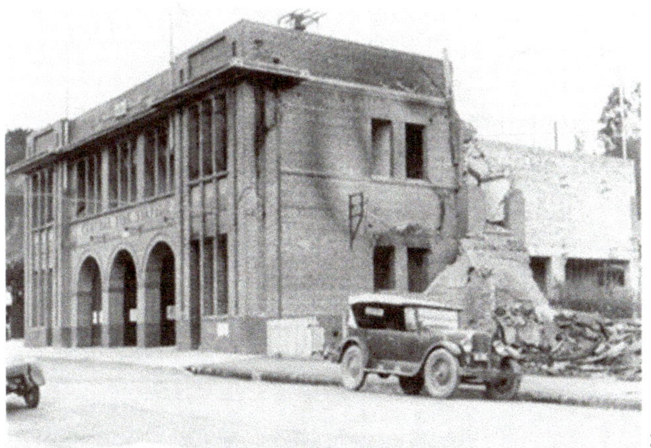

30

---

30 "Central Fire Station, Napier," gifted by H J Williams, collection of Hawke's Bay Museums Trust, Ruawharo Tā-ū-rangi, W121(c).

Memorable events in April:

On the 5th of April 1855, the first sale of town sections occurred comprising 108 lots consisting of 36-acre sections on Meeanee Spit, 58-acre sections on Scinde Island and across at the harbour 14 suburban sections of 13 to 39 acres @ £5 per quarter-acre.

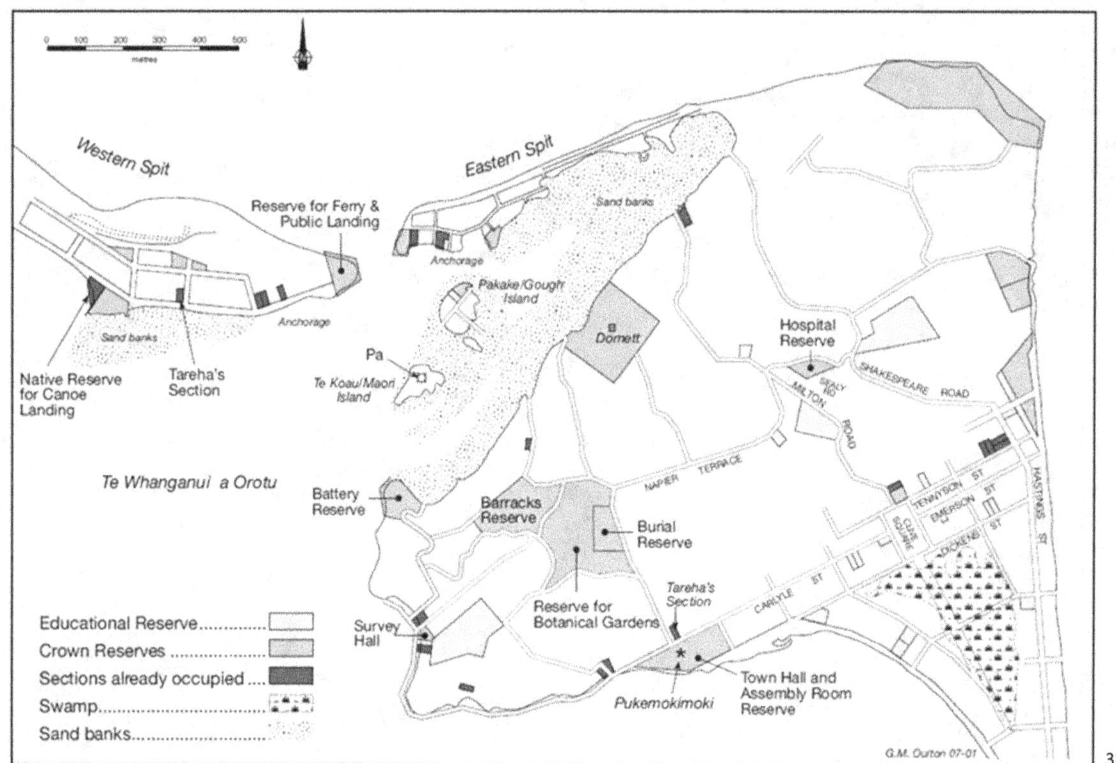

In April 1859, the first provincial council elections were held.

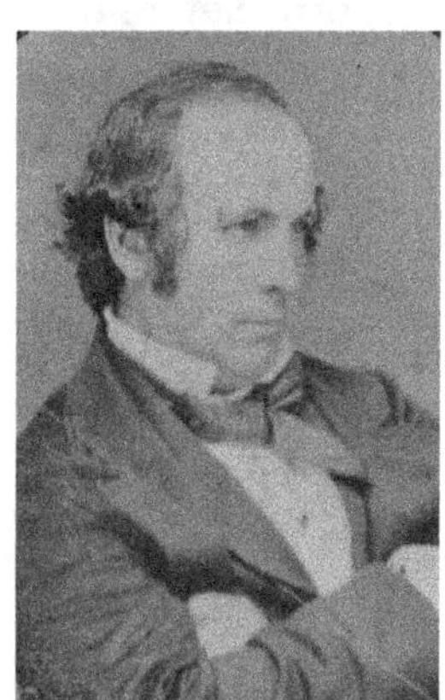

Thomas Henry Fitzgerald was a key mover in the separation of the Hawke's Bay area from the Wellington Province, and after the formation of the Hawke's Bay Province on 1 November 1858 became its first Superintendent from April 1859 to March 1861. He had previously represented the Ahuriri electorate on the Wellington Provincial Council from November 1857 to November 1858.

At the same time, he represented the Town of Napier electorate on the Hawke's Bay Provincial Council from February 1859 to November 1861.

---

[31] Plan of Napier: Waitangi Tribunal Report Wai201. 2004.

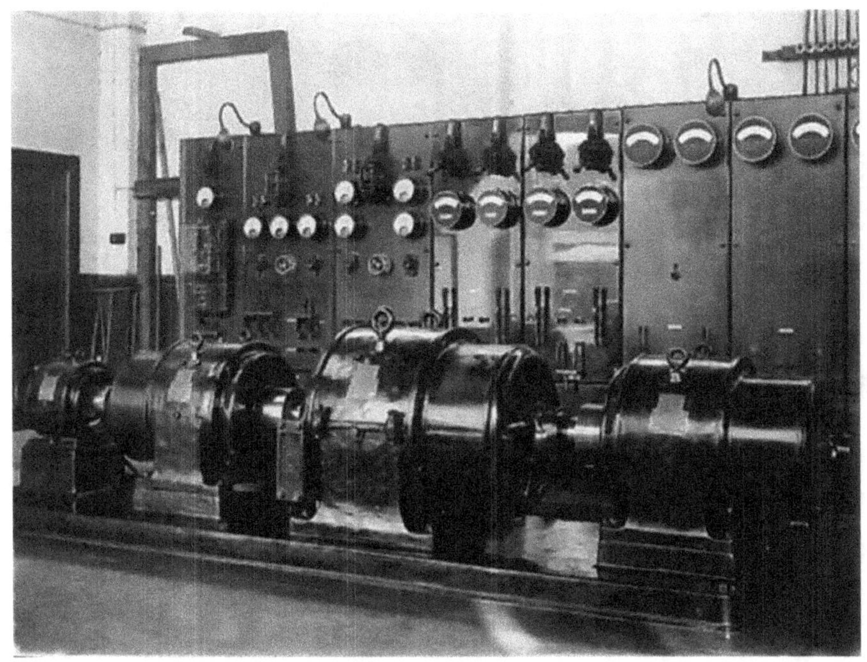

In April 1924 the Napier Council, together with the HB County Council and the Taradale Town Board, agreed to form the Hawkes Bay Electric Power Board to control the distribution of electricity to local authorities and private consumers.

Napier Municipal Power Station[32]

On 1 April 1968 Taradale amalgamated with Napier.

The name Taradale originated when an Irish immigrant Henry Alley leased a lot in the area in 1858, and a subsequent subdivision and township was created which he supposedly named after the Hill of Tara in County Meath in Ireland. Taradale was also the name of a small town in Victoria, Australia where he had previously lived until he emigrated to New Zealand in the late 1850s. The Victorian town Taradale had been named by a colonial surveyor after the Scottish town of Tarradale.

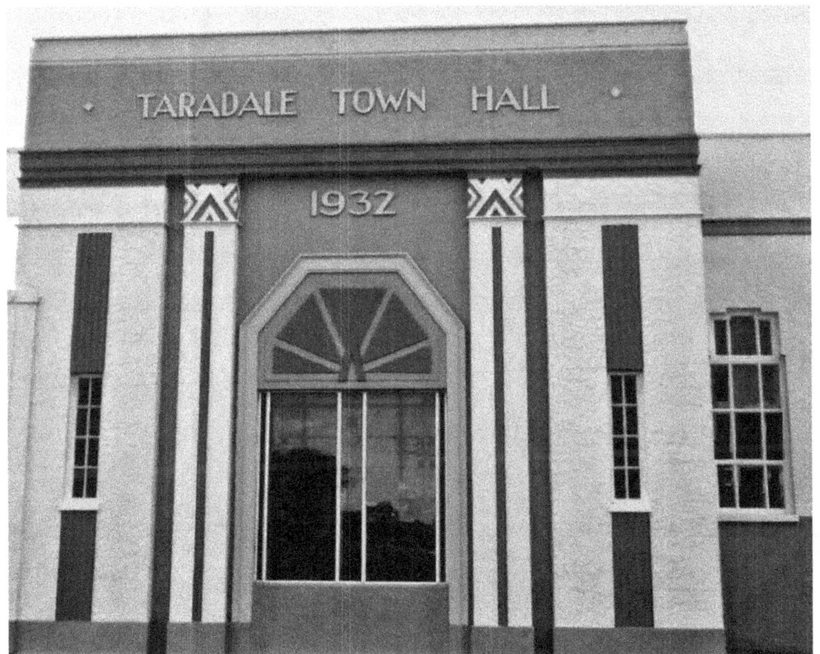

Taradale established a Town Board in 1886 and was part of the Hawke's Bay County Council. It became a borough in 1953.

The Taradale Town Hall at 8 Meeanee Road was designed by the architect EA Williams, and built by George H Wilson. It was completed in 1932, and its style is described as Art Deco.

---

[32] Photo by Leslie Adkin, March 1922. Gift of G. L. Adkin family estate, 1964. Te Papa Collection.

1	2	3	4
5	6	7	8
9	10	11	12
13	14	15	16
17	18	19	20
21	22	23	24
25	26	27	28
29	30		

May

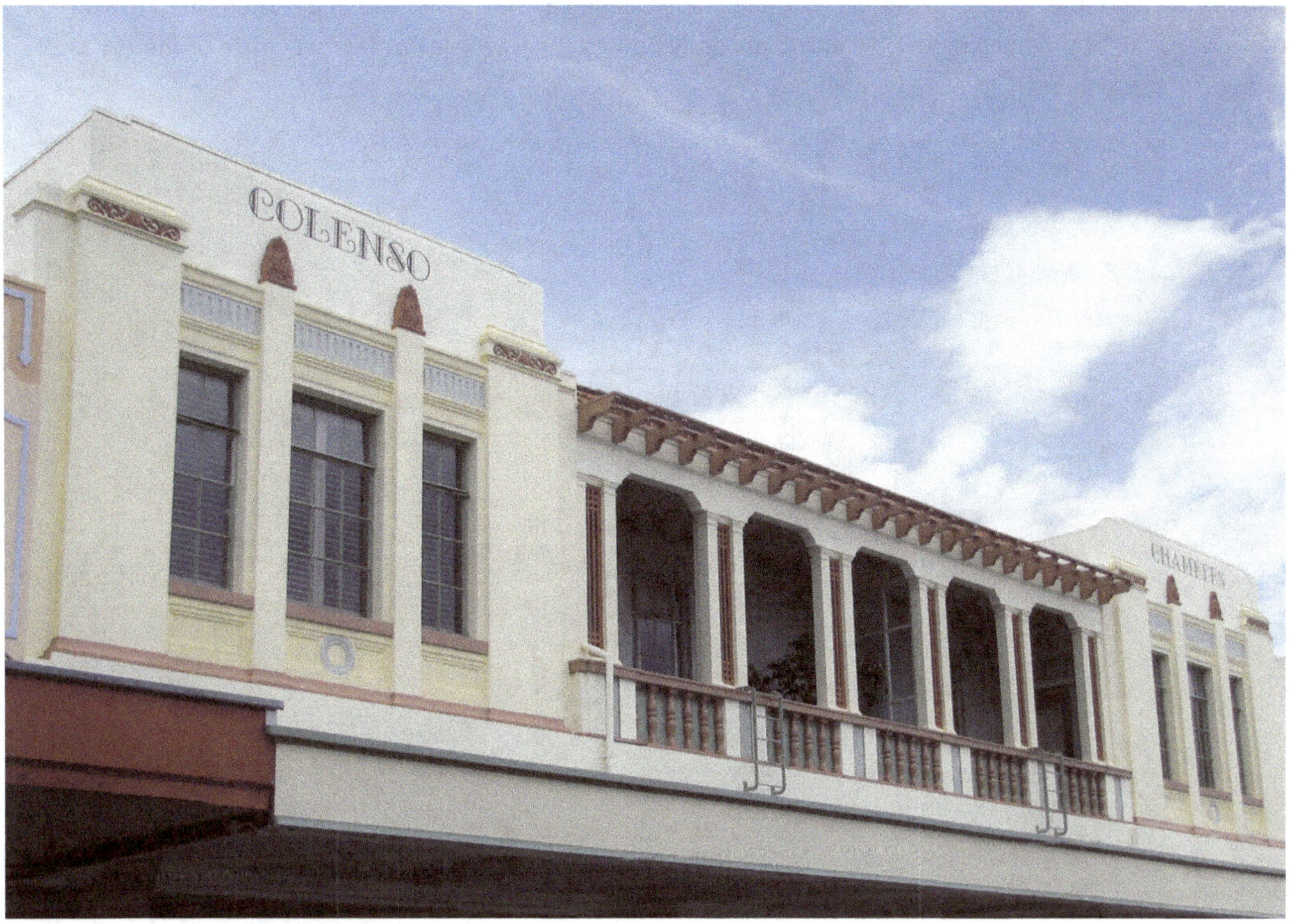

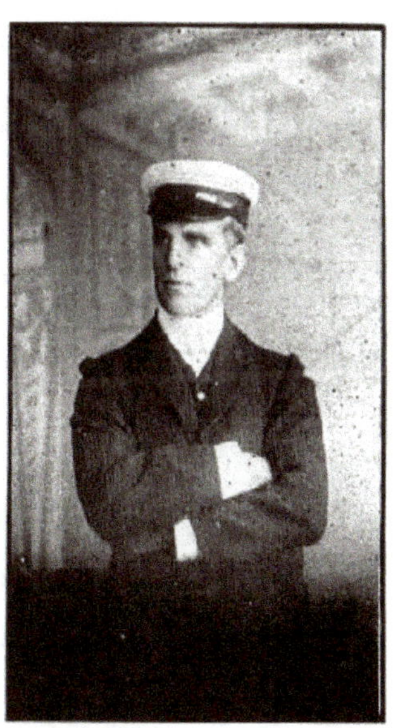

The Colenso building's architect was E.A. Williams and the builder was Holder Bros. The building was completed in 1932. Its style is described as Spanish Mission. The original use was as a private hotel called the Arcadia before the earthquake, and was rebuilt as the County Hotel. It has been known for many years as the Colenso Chambers.

FW Triggs and the J. Hindmarsh estate were the owners of the original building. Mr FW Triggs was also the captain of the Napier Sailing Club.

Mr. F. W. Triggs.

Memorable events in May

The Napier Courthouse at 59 Marine Parade opened in May 1875. The Department of Conservation bought the building in 1989 and it currently houses the Hawke's Bay District Office of the Department.

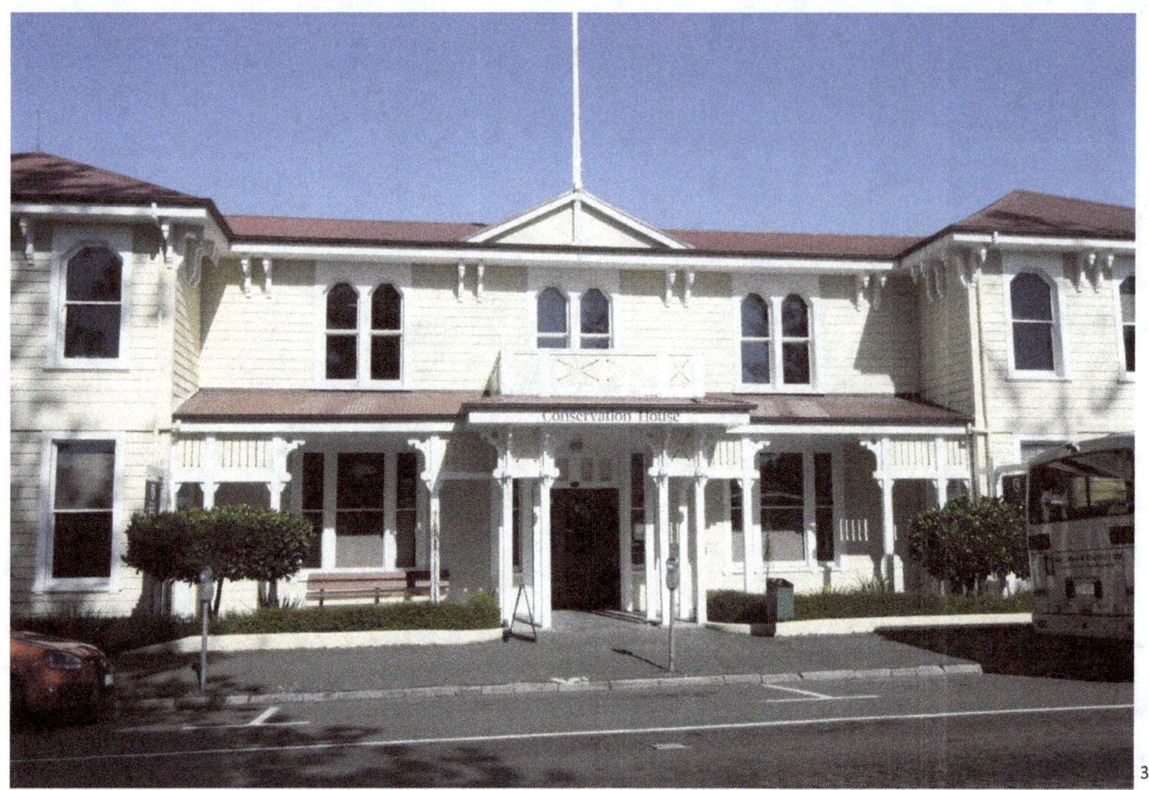

In May 1877, the Napier Theatre Company was founded.

A meeting of the Theatre Company was held at the Criterion Hotel last night, the attendance being small. Dr Gibbes was voted to the chair. Mr Upham briefly explained that 67 shares had been taken since the last meeting, making in all 100 shares subscribed for. A resolution was passed that a committee be appointed to inspect a few of the best sites in Napier for the proposed theatre, and to ascertain the prices, the same to be submitted to a meeting of shareholders prior to the signing of the deed of association. The following sites were mentioned, with the prices quoted :—A site in Shakespeare-road for £2000 ; one in Shakespeare-quarry, 90 feet by 180 feet, £600 ; one adjoining the HERALD office, 60 feet by 125 feet, £1000 ; and one 66 feet by 165 feet, with frontages to Emerson-street and Tennyson-street, £750.

---

[33] Photo by Bruce Tuten from Savannah, Georgia, United States - CC BY 2.0 via Wikimedia Commons

[34] Excerpt from the Hawkes Bay Herald, 13 June 1877 - National Library of NZ - Papers Past

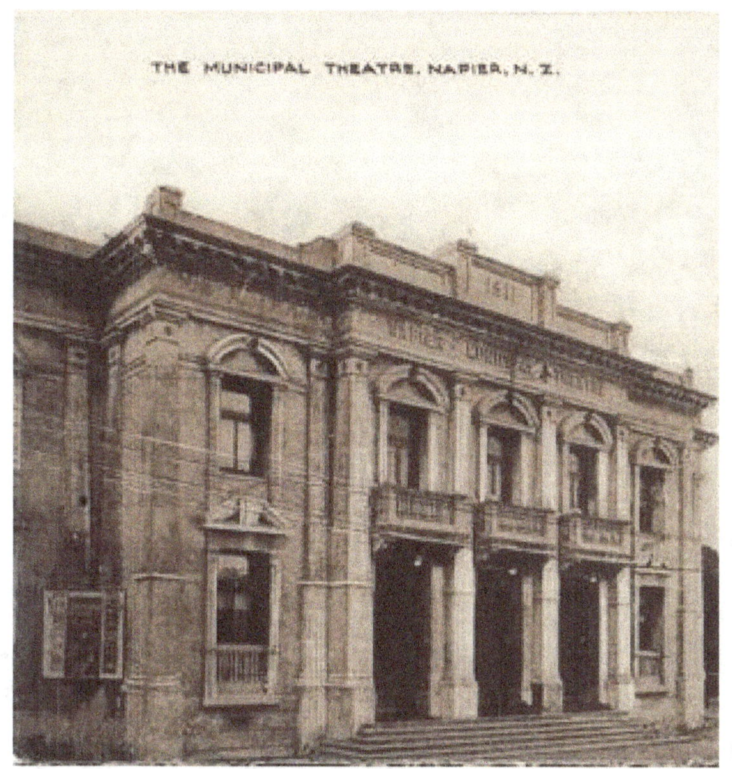

The Municipal Theatre in Napier

Performances were held in the Napier Municipal Theatre from 1912. This building was designed in the Italian Renaissance style by the Australian architect William Pitt. The building was severely damaged in the Napier earthquake, and plans for its replacement were drawn up in 1935. Nearby Clive Square was a common meeting place in Napier before performances.

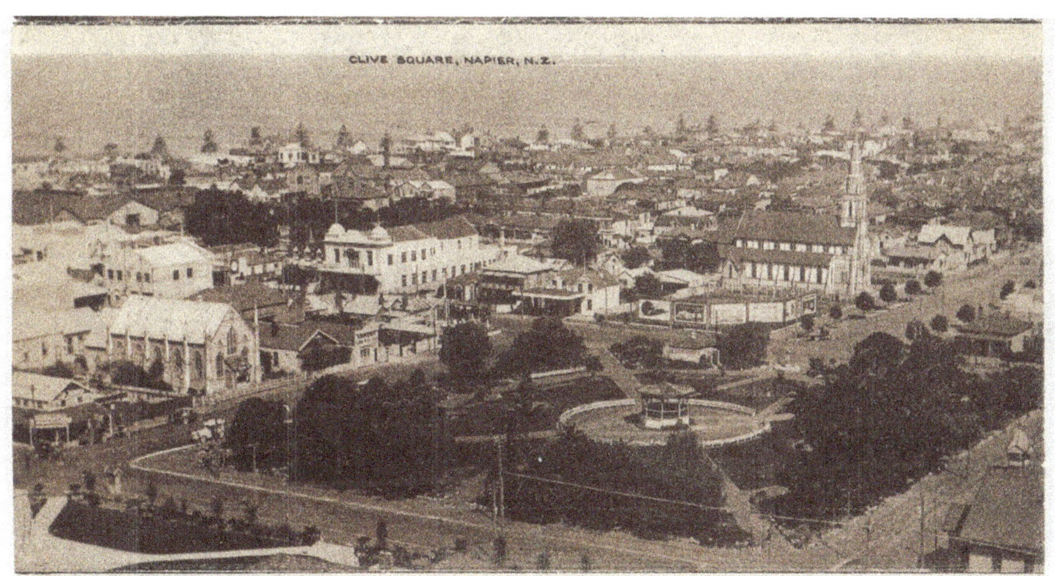

---

[35] Source: Unknown photographer circa 1926. Te Papa Collection.

[36] Clive Square, Napier, N.Z., circa 1926, Napier, maker unknown. Te Papa Collection (O.041732)

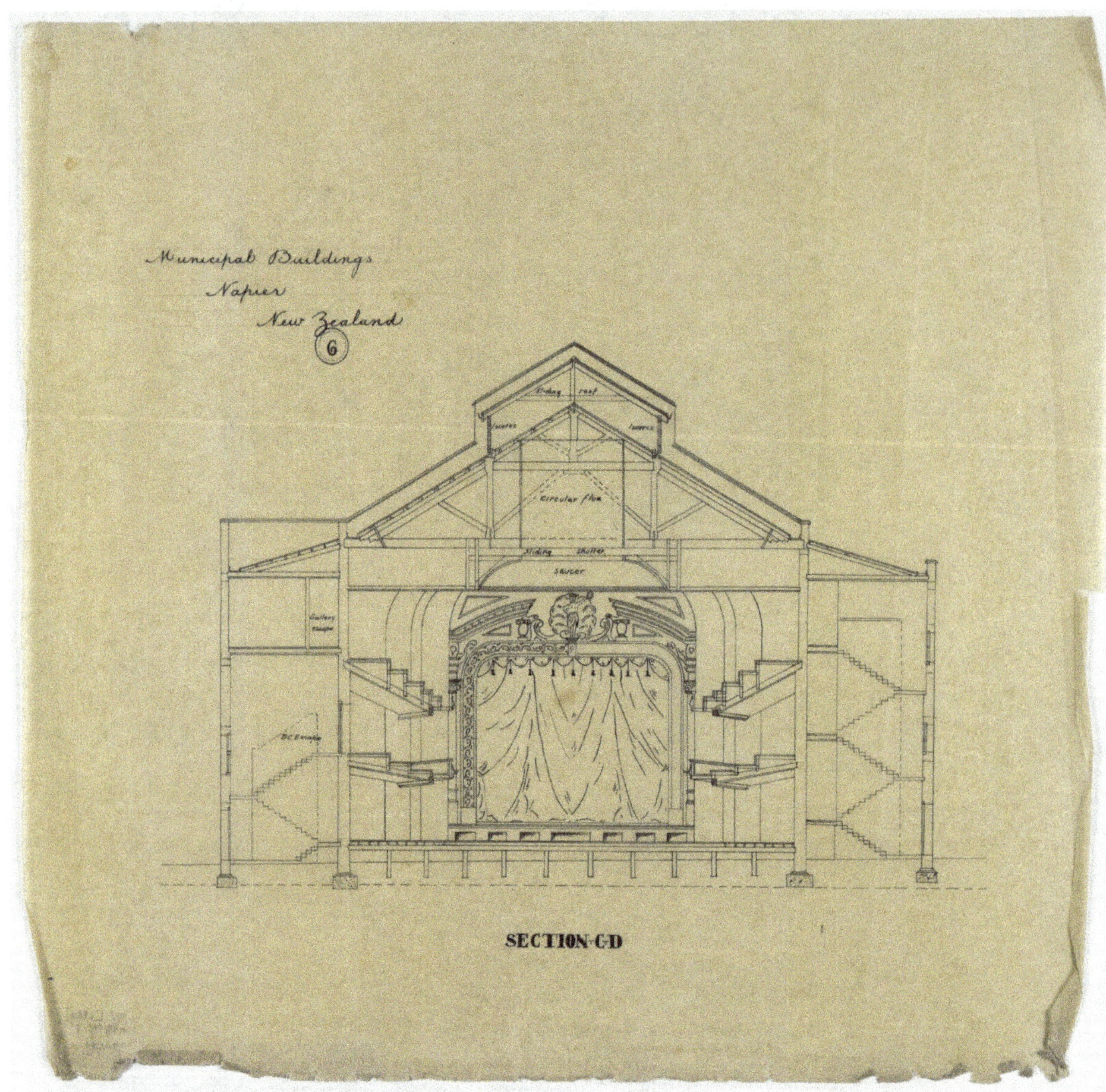

An architectural plan of the proposed new Municipal Theatre in Napier dated 17 Feb 1935 by the noted architect James Augustus Louis Hay (b.1881, d.1948).[37]

---

[37] Drawing gifted by Margaret Hay, collection of Hawke's Bay Museums Trust, Ruawharo Tā-ū-rangi, m82/33

In May 2013, the Hawke's Bay Museum & Art Gallery staff and collection began their move into their new home, and the transformation into MTG Hawke's Bay.

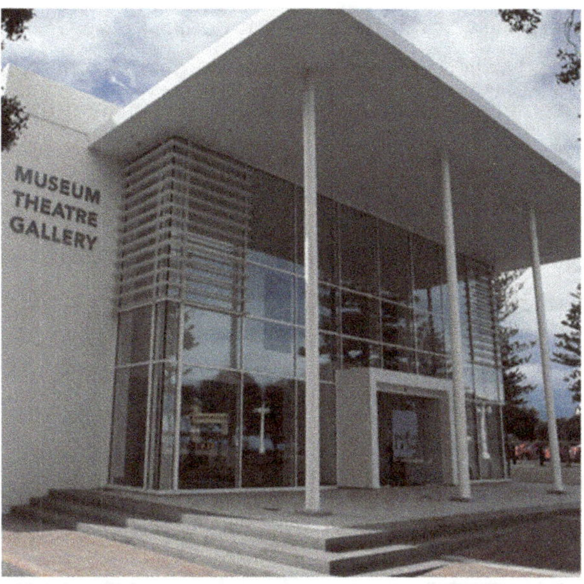

The original entrance of the Hawke's Bay Museum and Art Gallery was restored as part of the redevelopment into the new MTG complex.

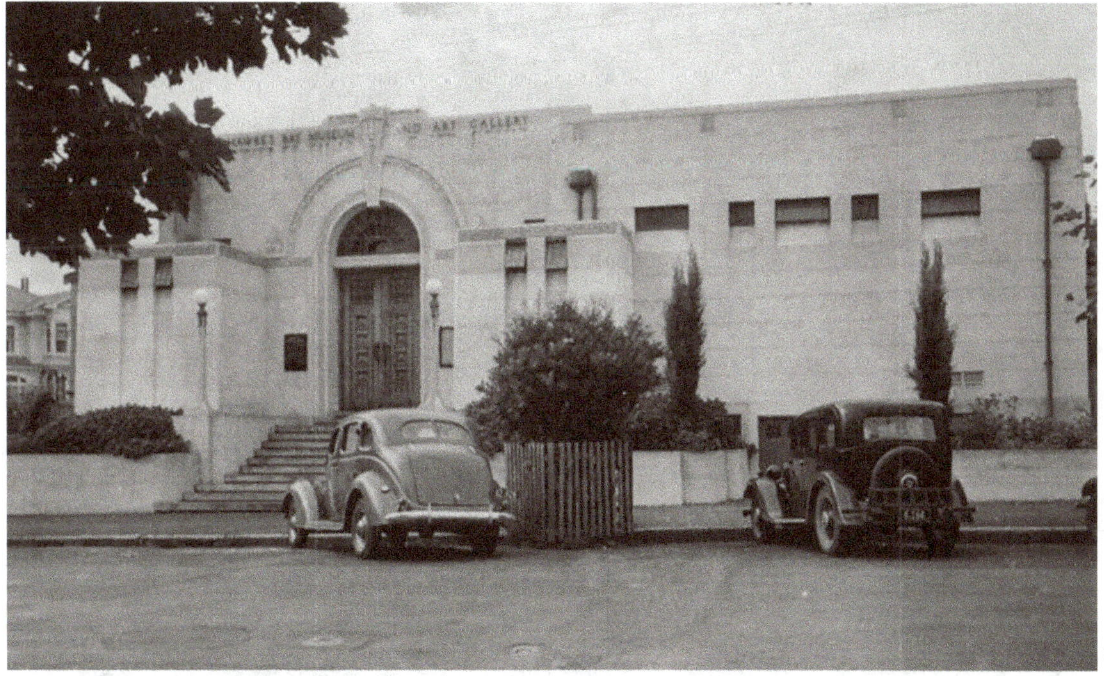

Original entrance to the Hawke's Bay Museum and Art Gallery

The predecessor organisations were the Mechanics Institute (1859), the Athenaeum (1865), the Philosophical Society (1874), the Napier Society of Arts and Crafts (1924), the Hawke's Bay Art

---

[38] "Hawke's Bay Museum and Art Gallery, 1936-1944," collection of Hawke's Bay Museums Trust, Ruawharo Tā-ū-rangi, 1838

Gallery and Museum (1936), Hawke's Bay Museum (1989), the Hawke's Bay Museum & Art Gallery (2006) and now the MTG Hawke's Bay (2013).

The Mechanics Institutes were based on the equivalent bodies in the UK. They provided lectures on science for local craftsmen and skilled workers (otherwise known as mechanics). The lectures also developed into "self-improvement" areas. An "Athenaeum" is an institution for the promotion of literary or scientific learning. These organisations generally provided extensive collections of books and reading rooms.

The objectives of these organisations are incorporated in the Napier Athenaeum and Mechanics Institute Incorporation Act of 1876:

> *"The objects and purposes of the body corporate shall be to aid and promote public education and moral and intellectual improvement, and the general study and cultivation of the various branches and departments of art science and literature, by means of libraries lectures, classes or in any similar manner, and to provide funds for such purposes, but the members of such body corporate shall not derive any personal pecuniary profit therefrom. "*

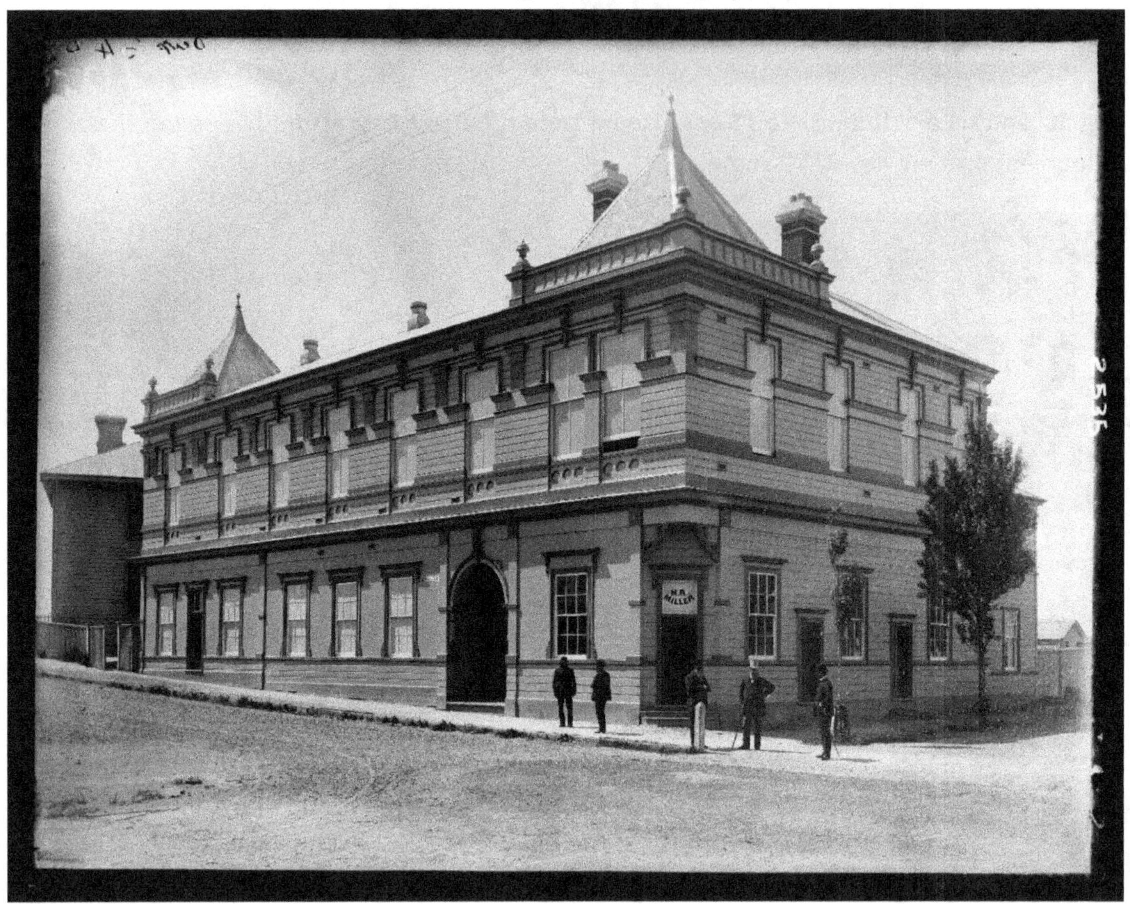

The Athenaeum building, Napier

---

[39] Photograph by Burton Brothers studio, maker unknown. Te Papa Collection - C.012535.

1	2	3	4
5	6	7	8
9	10	11	12
13	14	15	16
17	18	19	20
21	22	23	24
25	26	27	28
29	30	31	

June

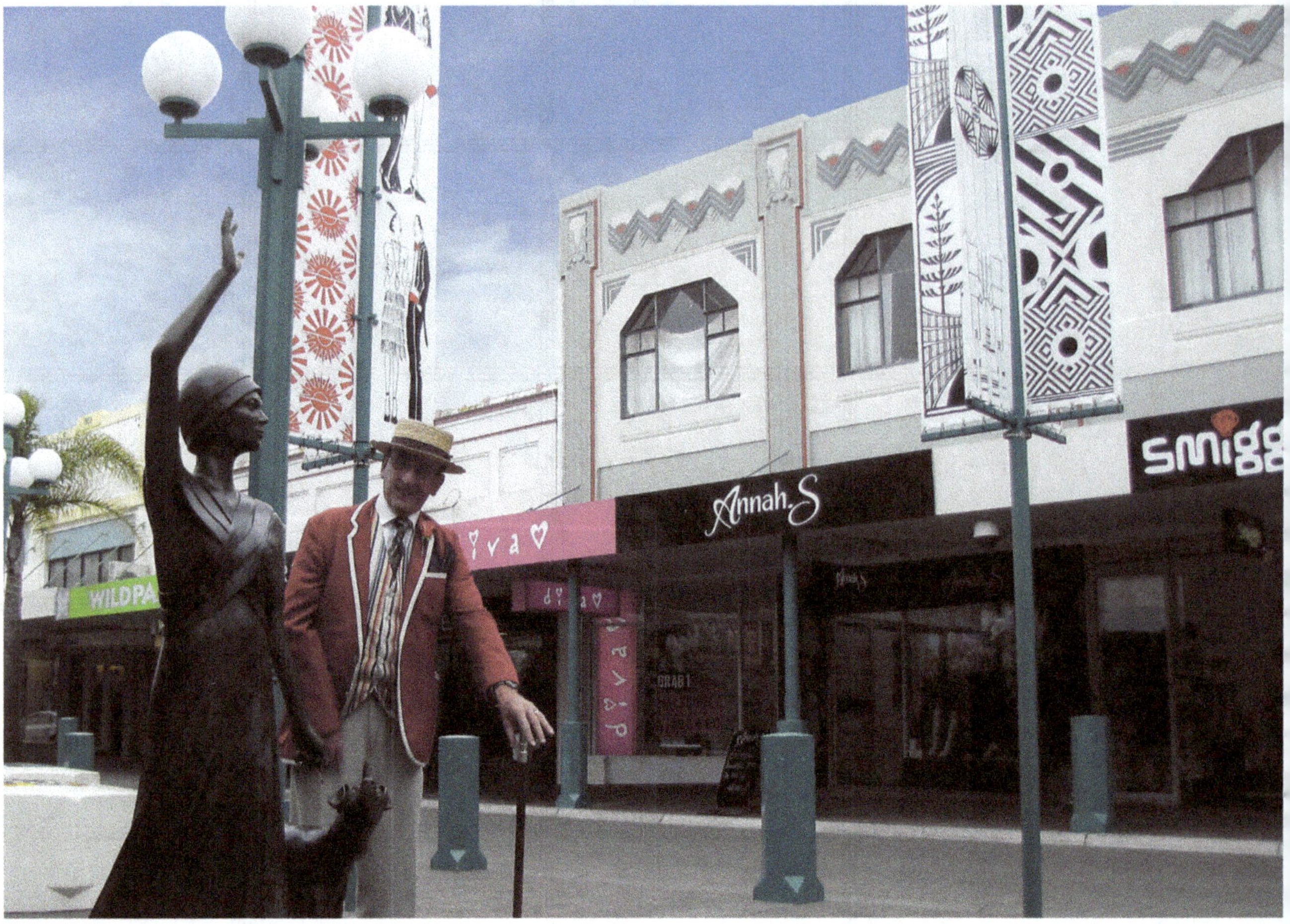

The Smith & Chambers building was completed in 1932. The architect was H Alfred Hill of Napier and the builder was the Fletcher Construction Company. Its style is described as Art Deco.

In the foreground, the bronze statue alongside one of the Art Deco volunteers in Napier was created by Mark Whyte of Lyttleton. It is called *"A Wave in Time."* The statue was commissioned by the Napier City Council in 2009 and unveiled in February 2010. The statue is modelled on Miss Sheila Williams, daughter of E.A. Williams who was one of the notable architects of the era. Miss Williams led the week long "New Napier Carnival" in January 1933 to celebrate the town's recovery from the earthquake. Her dog is called Raven.

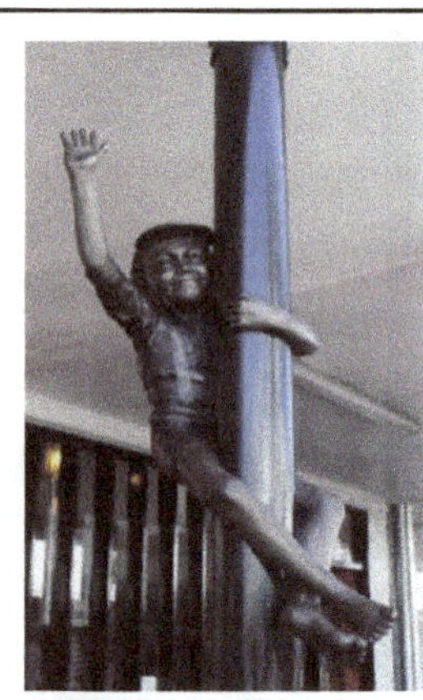

For some time since 2010, people had wondered who the lady was waving to. In 2014 a further bronze statue by the sculptor Mark Whyte was unveiled of a little boy climbing a pole and waving back from across the street.

Memorable events in June:

[From the *Hawke's Bay Herald*, June 24.]

IT is a painful duty that devolves upon us this morning—that of recording the loss of the ship Royal Bride during a fearful Nor'-east gale with which Hawke's Bay was visited on the night of Sunday last.

The gale, while it lasted, was (from that quarter) of strength unprecedented in the memory—not certainly of the oldest inhabitant, for traditionary accounts have been handed down, by old whalers and others, of black nor' easters such as that which has just been experienced—but certainly within the recollection of settlers of several years' standing. The wind-guage at the meteorological station indicated a maximum pressure of 25lbs ; and when it is recollected that 12lbs. denotes a storm, and 31lbs a hurricane, strong enough to tear up trees and carry all before it, some idea may be formed of the strength of the wind on Sunday night. From 7 p.m. there were strong and fitful gusts from N.E. by E. to E.N.E. with rain. At 9 p.m., the wind was fast increasing, and at midnight the gale was at its height. The sea rose rapidly, and was seen from the ill-fated vessel breaking right across the roadstead from the Bluff to Bluff. The bay is represented as having assumed the appearance of a sheet of fire.

On 10 June 1863, the first ship with passengers from London arrived at Napier. It was the Royal Bride, a ship of 526 tons with 24 assisted immigrants. She took 110 days to sail to Auckland, leaving the UK on January 9, 1863, and arriving in Auckland on April 29. She remained in Auckland until the end of May discharging cargo, before sailing for Napier. Unfortunately, the ship was lost in a heavy gale in July 1863, running aground between Petane and Napier about two miles from the entrance to the harbour.

Source: National Library of New Zealand Papers Past

In June 1889, a concrete wall was completed along Marine Parade as can be seen in this picture.

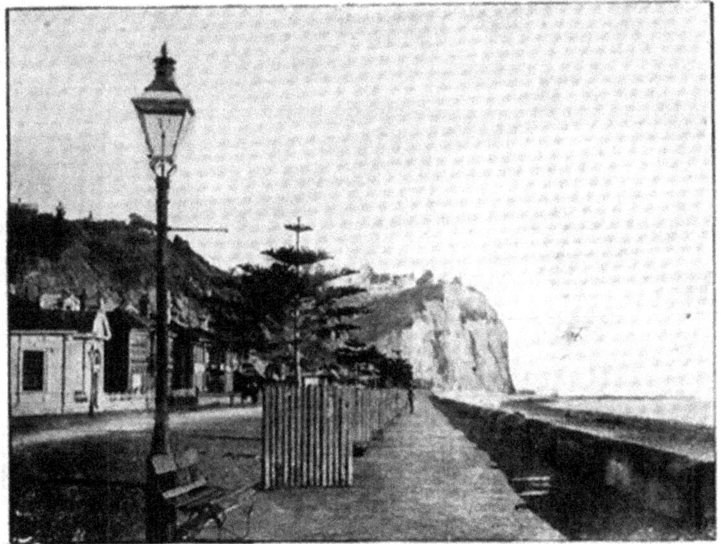

Esplanade and Bluff Hill, Napier[40]

---

[40] "Esplanade and Bluff Hill" by Cyclopedia Ltd, The New Zealand Electronic Text Collection (CC BY-SA).

The last tram rails were lifted from Napier streets in June 1937 (and the Council discontinued tram services permanently October 1935).

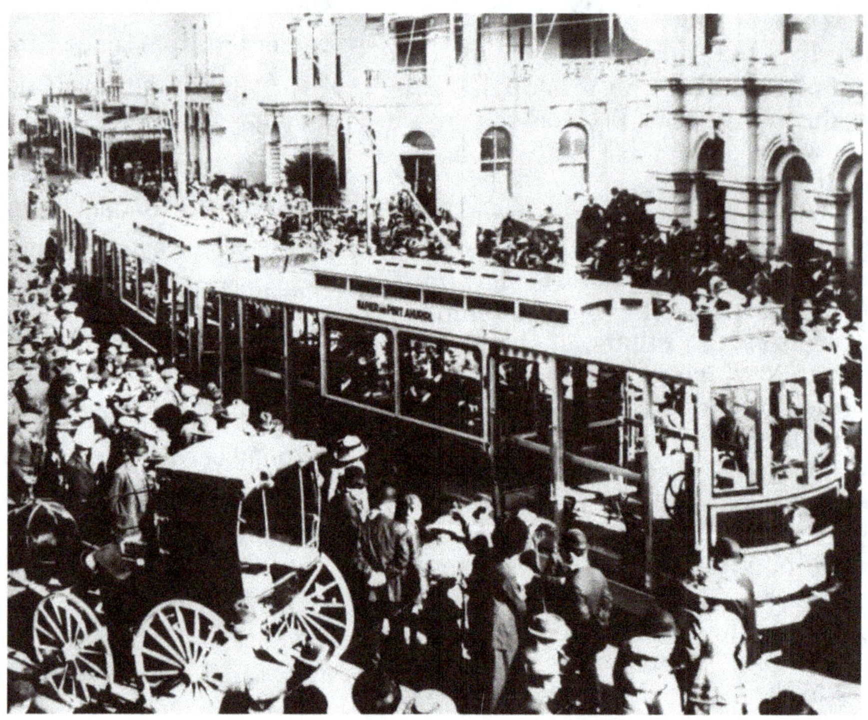

Photo: Opening the Tramway in 1912[41]

The Napier Municipal Theatre, an 1154 seat theatre was rebuilt and opened for its first performance on 3 June 1938 by a local company, the Napier Frivolity Minstrels.

The next performance was by the Napier Operatic Society with their production of "Rio Rita" a 1927 stage musical.[42]

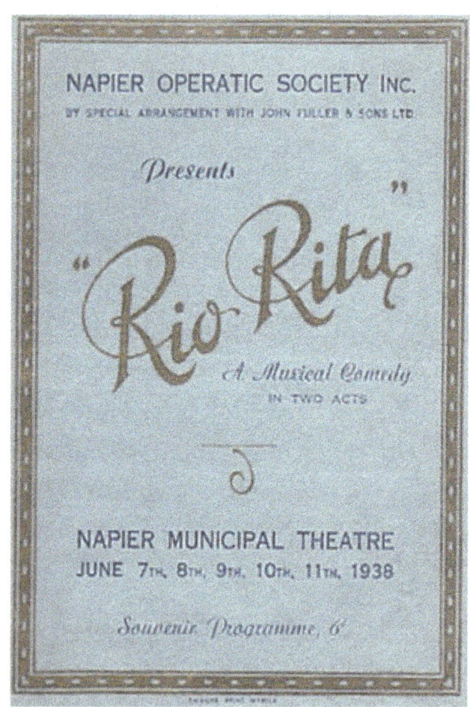

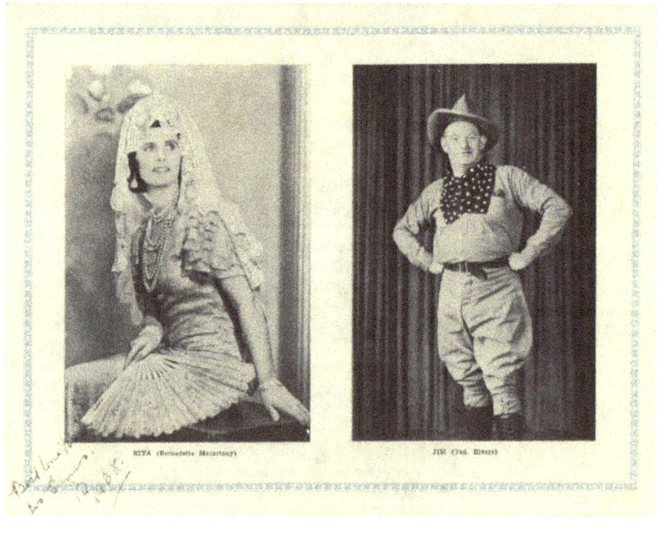

---

[41] Photo by R Pearcy, 1912, used with permission by Knowledge Bank - HB Digital Archives Trust www.knowledgebank.org.nz

[42] Pages from original programme. Own collection.

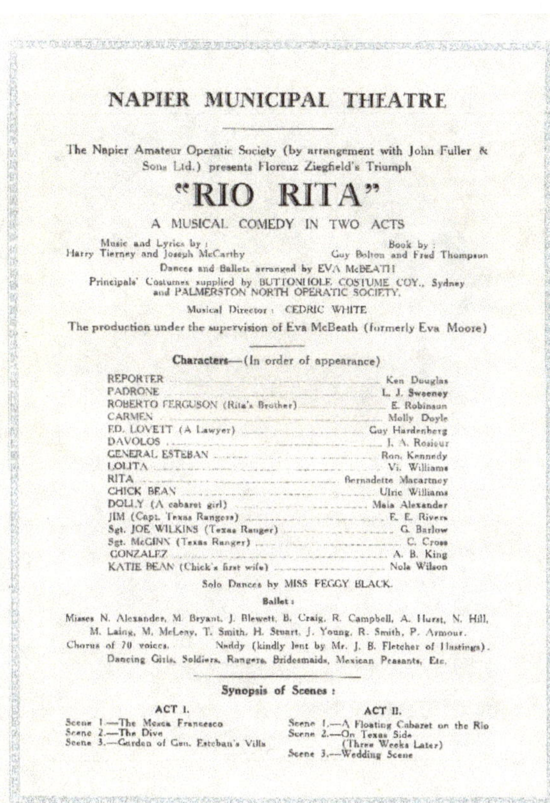

NAPIER MUNICIPAL THEATRE

The Napier Amateur Operatic Society (by arrangement with John Fuller & Sons Ltd.) presents Florenz Ziegfield's Triumph

"RIO RITA"

A MUSICAL COMEDY IN TWO ACTS

Music and Lyrics by :
Harry Tierney and Joseph McCarthy

Book by :
Guy Bolton and Fred Thompson

Dances and Ballets arranged by EVA McBEATH

Principals' Costumes supplied by BUTTONHOLE COSTUME COY., Sydney and PALMERSTON NORTH OPERATIC SOCIETY.

Musical Director : CEDRIC WHITE

The production under the supervision of Eva McBeath (formerly Eva Moore)

Characters—(In order of appearance)

REPORTER	Ken Douglas
PADRONE	L. J. Sweeney
ROBERTO FERGUSON (Rita's Brother)	E. Robinson
CARMEN	Molly Doyle
ED. LOVETT (A Lawyer)	Guy Hardenberg
DAVOLOS	J. A. Rosieur
GENERAL ESTEBAN	Ron. Kennedy
LOLITA	Vi. Williams
RITA	Bernadette Macartney
CHICK BEAN	Ulric Williams
DOLLY (A cabaret girl)	Maia Alexander
JIM (Capt. Texas Rangers)	E. E. Rivers
Sgt. JOE WILKINS (Texas Ranger)	G. Barlow
Sgt. McGINN (Texas Ranger)	C. Cross
GONZALEZ	A. B. King
KATIE BEAN (Chick's first wife)	Nola Wilson

Solo Dances by MISS PEGGY BLACK.

Ballet :

Misses N. Alexander, M. Bryant, J. Blewett, B. Craig, R. Campbell, A. Hurst, N. Hill, M. Laing, M. McLeay, T. Smith, H. Stuart, J. Young, R. Smith, P. Armour.

Chorus of 70 voices. Neddy (kindly lent by Mr. J. B. Fletcher of Hastings).

Dancing Girls, Soldiers, Rangers, Bridesmaids, Mexican Peasants, Etc.

Synopsis of Scenes :

ACT I.
Scene 1.—The Mesca Francesco
Scene 2.—The Dive
Scene 3.—Garden of Gen. Esteban's Villa

ACT II.
Scene 1.—A Floating Cabaret on the Rio
Scene 2.—On Texas Side
(Three Weeks Later)
Scene 3.—Wedding Scene

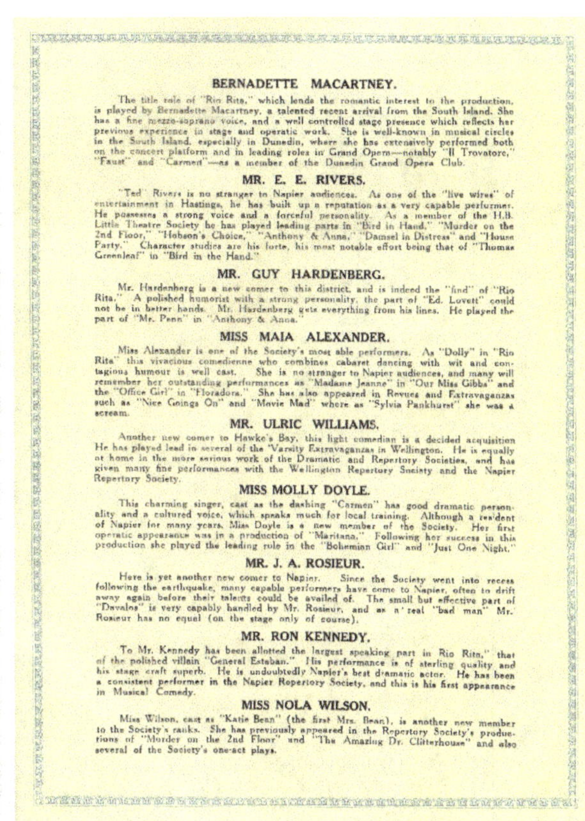

BERNADETTE MACARTNEY.

The title role of "Rio Rita," which lends the romantic interest to the production, is played by Bernadette Macartney, a talented recent arrival from the South Island. She has a fine mezzo-soprano voice, and a well controlled stage presence which reflects her previous experience in stage and operatic work. She is well-known in musical circles in the South Island, especially in Dunedin, where she has extensively performed both on the concert platform and in leading roles in Grand Opera—notably "Il Trovatore," "Faust" and "Carmen"—as a member of the Dunedin Grand Opera Club.

MR. E. E. RIVERS.

"Ted" Rivers is no stranger to Napier audiences. As one of the "live wires" of entertainment in Hastings, he has built up a reputation as a very capable performer. He possesses a strong voice and a forceful personality. As a member of the H.B. Little Theatre Society he has played leading parts in "Bird in Hand," "Murder on the 2nd Floor," "Hobson's Choice," "Anthony & Anna," "Damsel in Distress" and "House Party." Character studies are his forte, his most notable effort being that of "Thomas Greenleaf" in "Bird in the Hand."

MR. GUY HARDENBERG.

Mr. Hardenberg is a new comer to this district, and is indeed the "find" of "Rio Rita." A polished humorist with a strong personality, the part of "Ed. Lovett" could not be in better hands. Mr. Hardenberg gets everything from his lines. He played the part of "Mr. Penn" in "Anthony & Anna."

MISS MAIA ALEXANDER.

Miss Alexander is one of the Society's most able performers. As "Dolly" in "Rio Rita" this vivacious comedienne who combines cabaret dancing with wit and contagious humour is well cast. She is no stranger to Napier audiences, and many will remember her outstanding performances as "Madame Jeanne" in "Our Miss Gibbs" and the "Office Girl" in "Floradora." She has also appeared in Revues and Extravaganzas such as "Nice Goings On" and "Movie Mad" where as "Sylvia Pankhurst" she was a scream.

MR. ULRIC WILLIAMS.

Another new comer to Hawke's Bay, this light comedian is a decided acquisition. He has played lead in several of the 'Varsity Extravaganzas in Wellington. He is equally at home in the more serious work of the Dramatic and Repertory Societies, and has given many fine performances with the Wellington Repertory Society and the Napier Repertory Society.

MISS MOLLY DOYLE.

This charming singer, cast as the dashing "Carmen" has good dramatic personality and a cultured voice, which speaks much for local training. Although a resident of Napier for many years, Miss Doyle is a new member of the Society. Her first operatic appearance was in a production of "Maritana." Following her success in this production she played the leading role in the "Bohemian Girl" and "Just One Night."

MR. J. A. ROSIEUR.

Here is yet another new comer to Napier. Since the Society went into recess following the earthquake, many capable performers have come to Napier, often to drift away again before their talents could be availed of. The small but effective part of "Davalos" is very capably handled by Mr. Rosieur, and as n' real "bad man" Mr. Rosieur has no equal (on the stage only of course).

MR. RON KENNEDY.

To Mr. Kennedy has been allotted the largest speaking part in Rio Rita," that of the polished villain "General Esteban." His performance is of sterling quality and his stage craft superb. He is undoubtedly Napier's best dramatic actor. He has been a consistent performer in the Napier Repertory Society, and this is his first appearance in Musical Comedy.

MISS NOLA WILSON.

Miss Wilson, cast as "Katie Bean" (the first Mrs. Bean), is another new member to the Society's ranks. She has previously appeared in the Repertory Society's productions of "Murder on the 2nd Floor" and "The Amazing Dr. Clitterhouse" and also several of the Society's one-act plays.

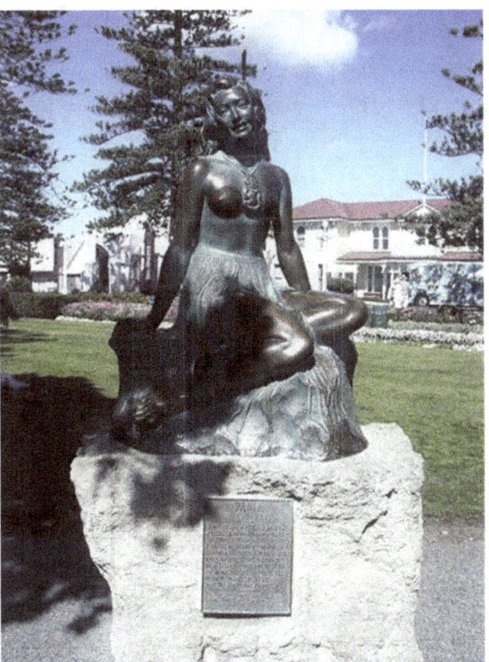

In June 1954 Pania of the Reef was unveiled as a gift from the Thirty Thousand Club. A Maori legend tells how Pania left her sea people to marry Karitoki, a local chieftain.

After Karitoki left to fight in a long tribal war, Pania's original family called to her at sunset and at dawn. Unable to resist their siren voices, she swam out to meet them. When she attempted to return to the shore, however, she was drawn down to the caverns of the sea.

Angered by her divided loyalties, Moana-nui-a-kiwa (lord of the sea) transformed her into a rocky shelf. Lying off the Napier breakwater, the beautiful sea creature is immortalised as Pania's Reef.

43

---

[43] "Pania of the Reef," by Paul Funnell

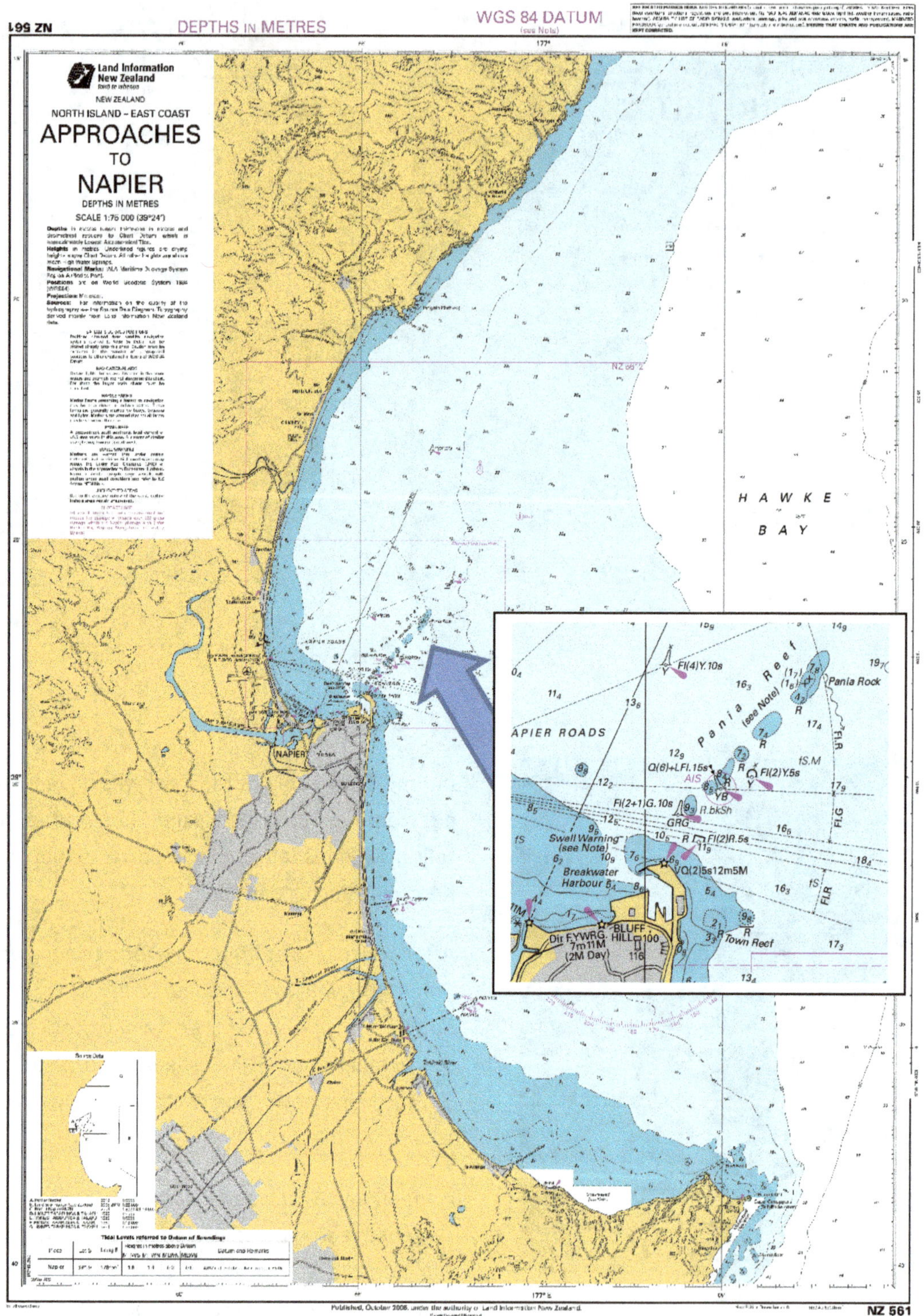

Napier coastal boating chart[44] showing the location of Pania Reef.

[44] Chart provided by Land Information NZ (LINZ) www.linz.govt.nz/sea/charts under Creative Commons 3.0 licence

1	2	3	4
5	6	7	8
9	10	11	12
13	14	15	16
17	18	19	20
21	22	23	24
25	26	27	28
29	30		

July

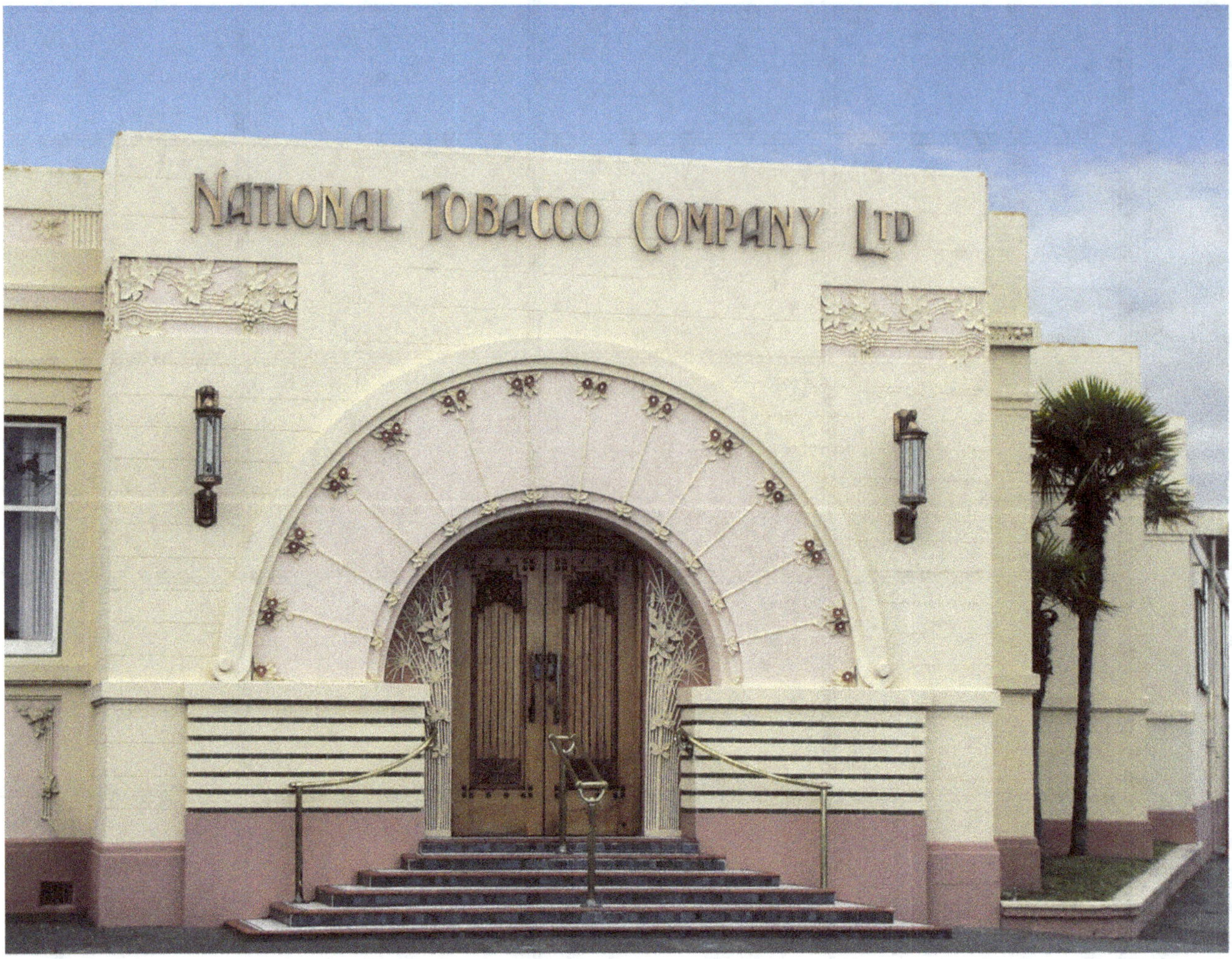

The architect for the new façade of the building after the 1931 earthquake was JA Louis Hay, and the builder was Faulknor Construction. It was completed in 1933. Its style is described as Chicago School.

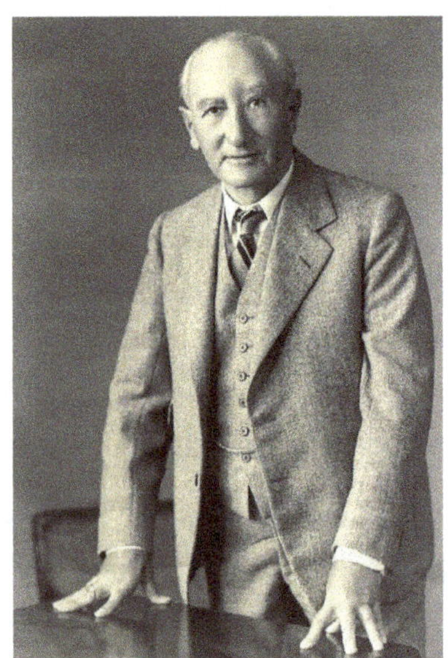

The original owner was Gerhard Husheer (Managing Director of the National Tobacco Company).

Gerhard Husheer emigrated to New Zealand in 1911 with plans to set up a tobacco industry. The family spent two years growing tobacco crops near Hastings and in 1913 formed the New Zealand Tobacco Company (a predecessor company to the National Tobacco Co formed in 1921). In the year 1915, he built a new processing factory at Ahuriri in Napier.

In the year 1957, it was sold to Rothmans, and was known as the 'Rothmans Building' until 2001 when the original name was reinstated with the original bronze letters.

Memorable events in July:

In July 1939, the Napier Sailing Club received permission to build a new clubhouse at "Scapa Flow" boat harbour (near West Quay at Ahuriri). Following the earthquake, the inner harbour changed so sailing had to be in the open sea.

Herald employes.

NAPIER SAILING CLUB.

Much interest is being taken by boating men in the opening of the Sailing Club's season to-morrow afternoon. The formation of the club seems to have been the means of infusing considerable life into yachting, and it is probable that a large number of boats will take part in to-morrow afternoon's proceedings. A procession of sailing crafts will leave the inner harbor at three o'clock, and with fine weather a pleasant few hours' sailing may be anticipated. The club now numbers forty-one members.

In connection with the opening of the Sailing Club's season in the inner harbor to-morrow afternoon, the Naval's cutter Beatrice will take part. As many of the crew as can possibly muster are requested to be at Fisherman's Bay at 2.30 p.m. sharp, in summer uniform. Major Wood and Captain Smith will also attend. The cutter will be in charge of C.P.O. Franklin.

BOWLING.

45

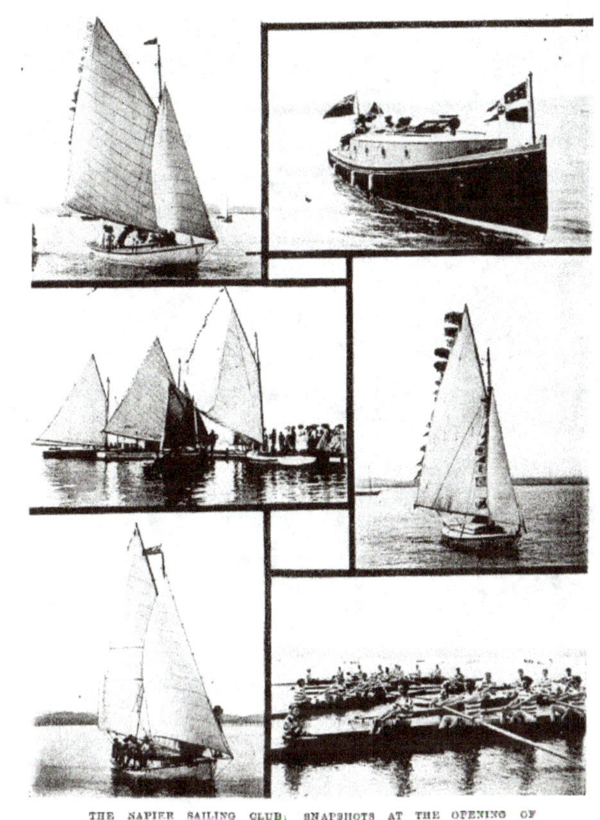

46

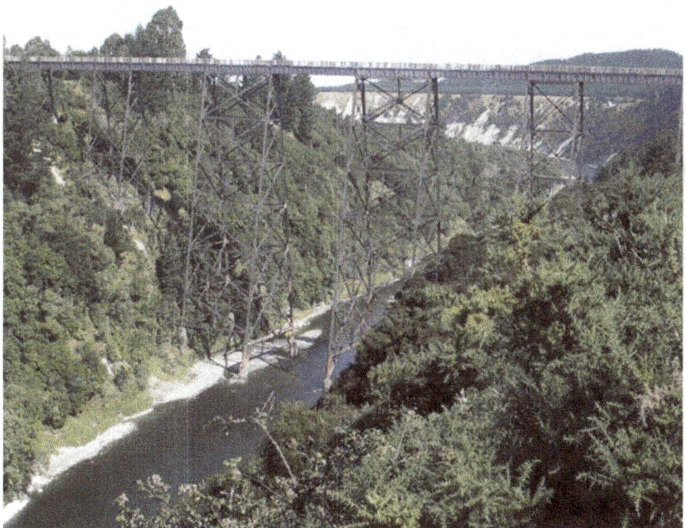

The official opening at Wairoa of the Napier-Wairoa railway was on 1 July, 1939. Trains cross the 97 metre-high Mohaka viaduct spanning the Mohaka River about half way between Napier and Wairoa. The bridge is of steel girder construction, is 270m long and was opened in 1937. It is now the tallest viaduct in Australasia. [47]

---

[45] "Napier Sailing Club Clipping" by the Daily Telegraph, 20 February 1891 from the National Library of New Zealand Papers Past.

[46] Photos from the Otago Witness, 7 December 1910. Source: National Library of New Zealand Papers Past

[47] "Mohaka viaduct from east" by Pinot, Wikimedia Commons (CC BY-SA).

In the month of July 1957, the Napier War Memorial was opened.

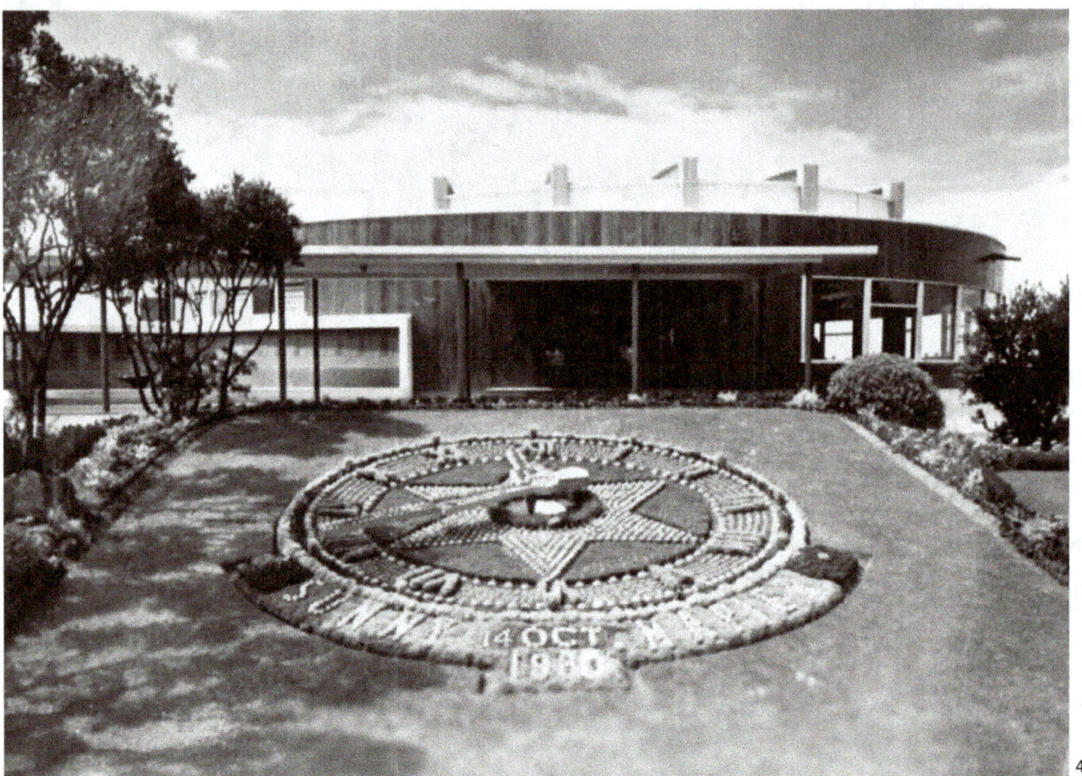

It is now the Napier Conference Centre and the war memorial features of the hall, including the eternal flame, have been relocated.

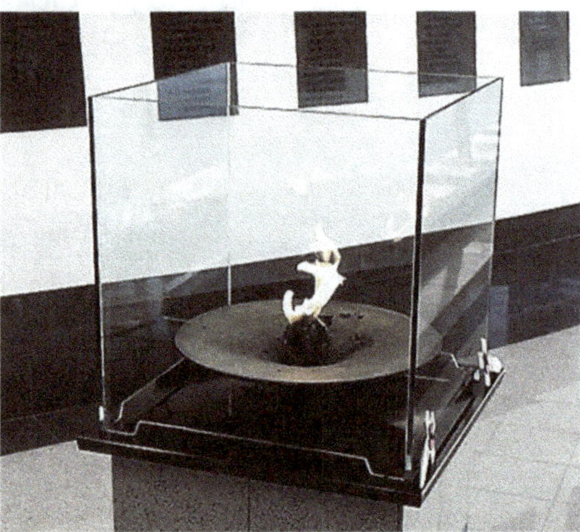

For many years the basement of the building housed the Napier aquarium and the main building area was occupied by a fine dining restaurant of the day called "La Ronde."

---

[48] Photo used with permission of Old Photos NZ www.oldphotos.co.nz

In July 1911, the citizens of Napier turned out on the streets to celebrate the Coronation of George V and Queen Mary at Westminster Abbey, London (on 22 June 1911).[49]

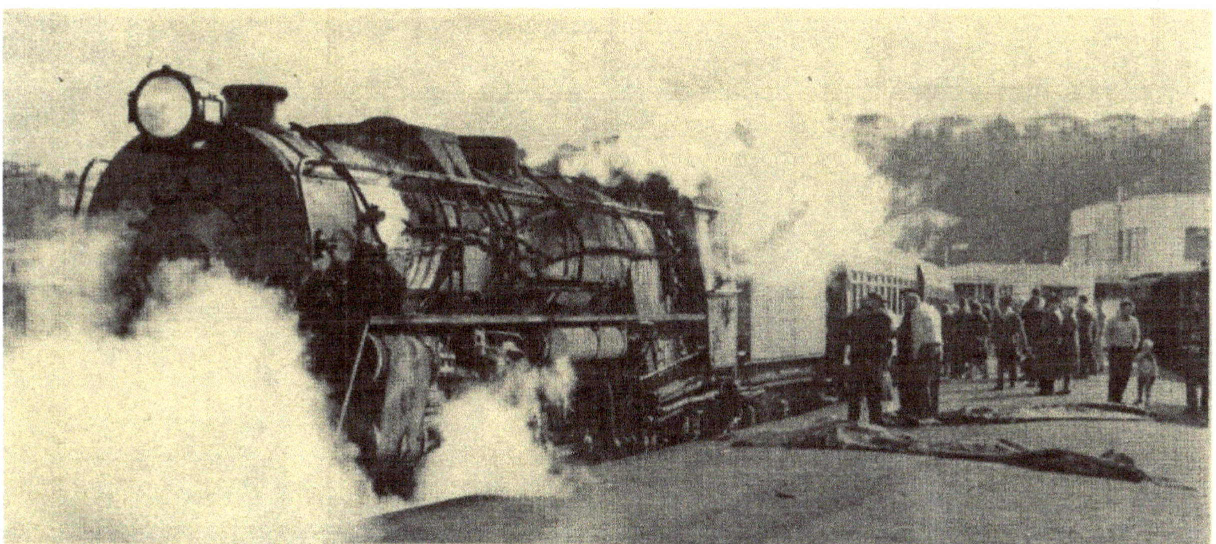

The last scheduled passenger steam train between Napier and Palmerston North left in July 1966.[50]

---

[49] Otago Witness, 5 July 1911. Source National Library of New Zealand Papers Past

[50] HB Photo News image July 1966. Used with permission by Knowledge Bank - HB Digital Archives Trust www.knowledgebank.org.nz

1	2	3	4
5	6	7	8
9	10	11	12
13	14	15	16
17	18	19	20
21	22	23	24
25	26	27	28
29	30	31	

August

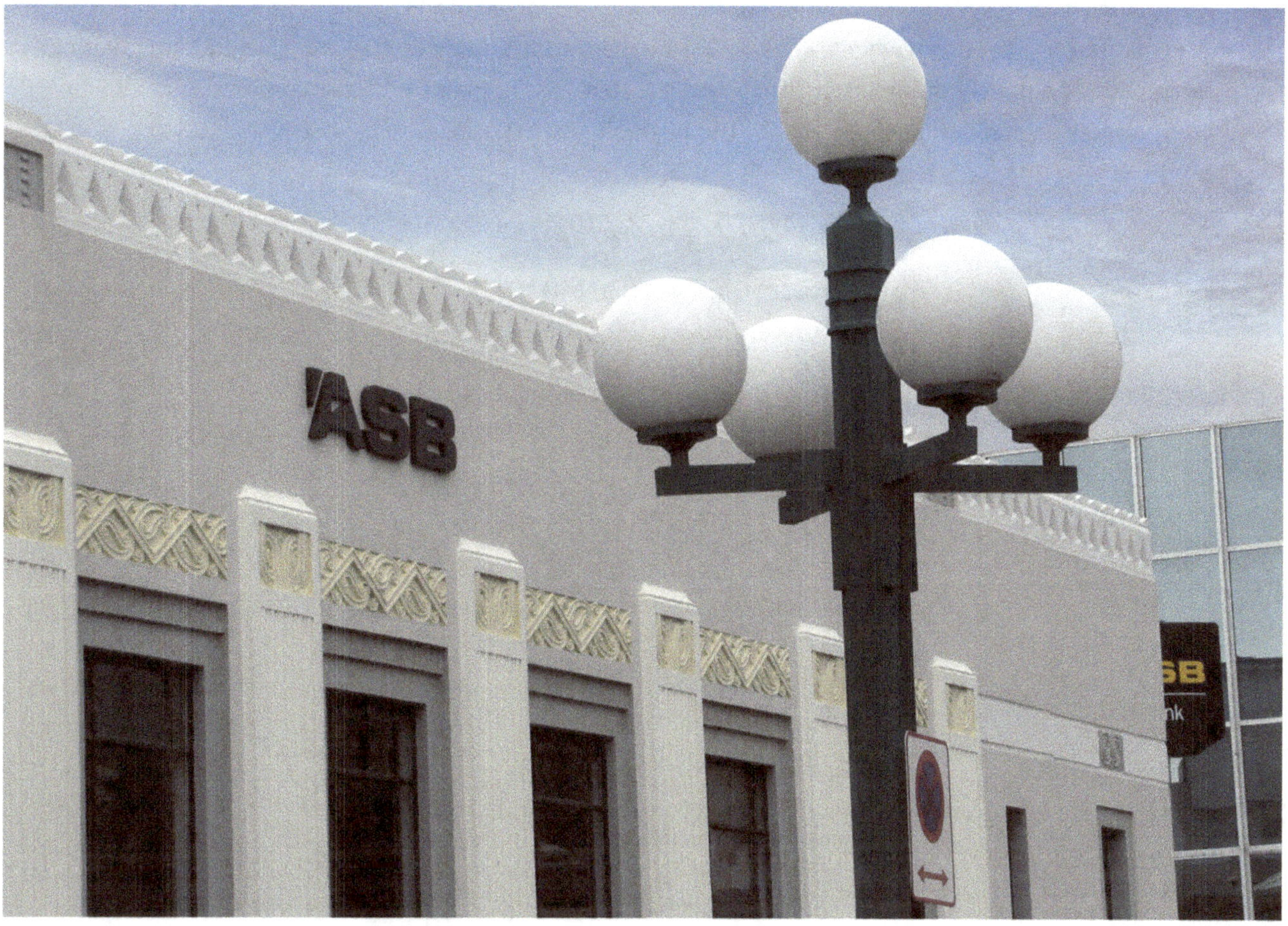

The architectural firm that designed the ASB building was Crichton, McKay & Haughton of Wellington. It was completed in 1932. Its style is described as Stripped Classical with Maori motifs

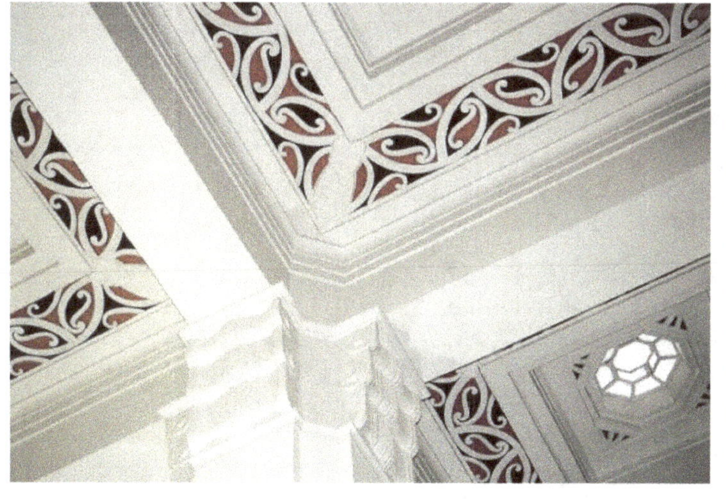

It has some other unique features including a Maori "Kowhaiwhai pattern" in red, black & white which forms a frieze around the top of the wall & ceiling bays. At the entrance to the building there are 2 corbels on either side representing "the wealth of the tribe." The exterior has combination Maori decoration with deco patterns.

Memorable events in August:

In August 1887 sixteen cases of typhoid fever were reported in the area of Enfield Road in Napier. It was stated that poor sewage disposal was the main contributing factor, and consequently typhoid remained a danger in Napier, Hastings and the Heretaunga Plains until the completion of swamp reclamation and drainage projects by the beginning of the 1900s.

TYPHOID IN NAPIER

Defective Sanitation

(By Telegraph—Press Association)

NAPIER, This Day.

The Borough Council sat last evening as a Board of Health to consider the report of Dr. Finch, acting District Health Officer for Hawke's Bay.

In his report, Dr Finch states that Napier is now undergoing its periodical course of typhoid, and that although searching investigation has been made, the absence of a common cause and the fact of the annual recurrence of the sickness shows it to be due to defective sanitation. This opinion is confirmed by the fact that nearly all the cases reported have come from the flat parts of the town, and houses where the pan system is in force.

He strongly advocates the appointment of a sanitary expert to inspect all plumbing work in connection with drainage and water-closet connections under proper specifications, and an amendment of the by-laws dealing with the same and with house ventilation. He also suggested the advisability of the establishment of a septic tank for the disposal of

sewage

The question of the amendment of the by-law in accordance with Dr Finch's report was left to be dealt with by the Council, which has already decided upon the appointment of an additional sanitary inspector.

Source: Wairarapa Daily Times, 25 March 1902. National Library of NZ – Papers Past

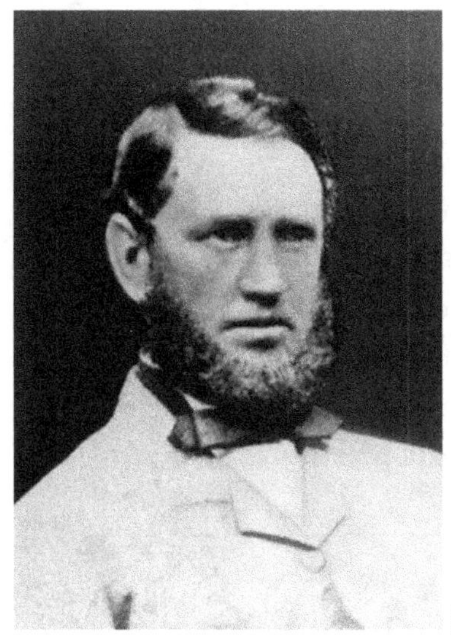

In August 1869 Robert Holt purchased two sections in Napier and a site for his business which was later to become Robert Holt & Sons.

Robert Holt.

Robert Holt was born at Oldham in England. He emigrated to New Zealand and arrived on the ship William Watson at Auckland on 8 February 1859. About 1872 he relocated his business from Emerson Street to Hastings Street and installed a steam- powered sawmill.

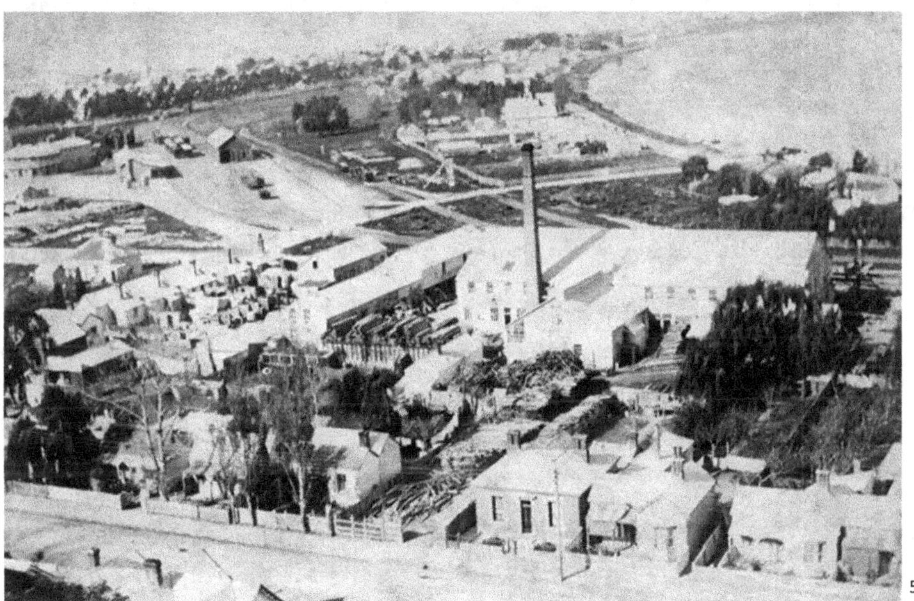

Sawmill in Napier - late 1800s

By 1880 he expanded his business to include a second steam sawmill at Port Ahuriri and in 1886 he established further operations on a two-acre site in Thackeray Street in Napier and built a sawmill near Dannevirke.

In 1910 the firm began trading under the name of Robert Holt and Sons. The firm became a limited liability company in 1929, and in 1971 the company (by now publicly listed) merged with Carter Consolidated to form Carter Holt Holdings.

---

[51] "Sawmill, Napier," collection of Hawke's Bay Museums Trust, Ruawharo Tā-ū-rangi, 2124.

On 5 August 1914 war was declared. Many soldiers from Hawke's Bay left to serve over the coming months, including the East Coast section of the Maori expeditionary force as can be seen in this send-off ceremony on the Marine Parade in Napier. [52]

The names of 300 fallen soldiers from the area killed in World War One are recorded in memorials in Hawke's Bay. There are many memorials to service in the region. Russell Street is Hastings for instance is named after Napier-born, Sir Andrew Russell, who commanded the New Zealand soldiers in World War One in England, Gallipoli, France and Belgium. Gallipoli Road and Flanders Avenue in Napier are other examples. The national "Places of Remembrance Project" and the Poppy Places Trust is creating memorials across New Zealand using commemorative poppies (poppyplaces.nz).

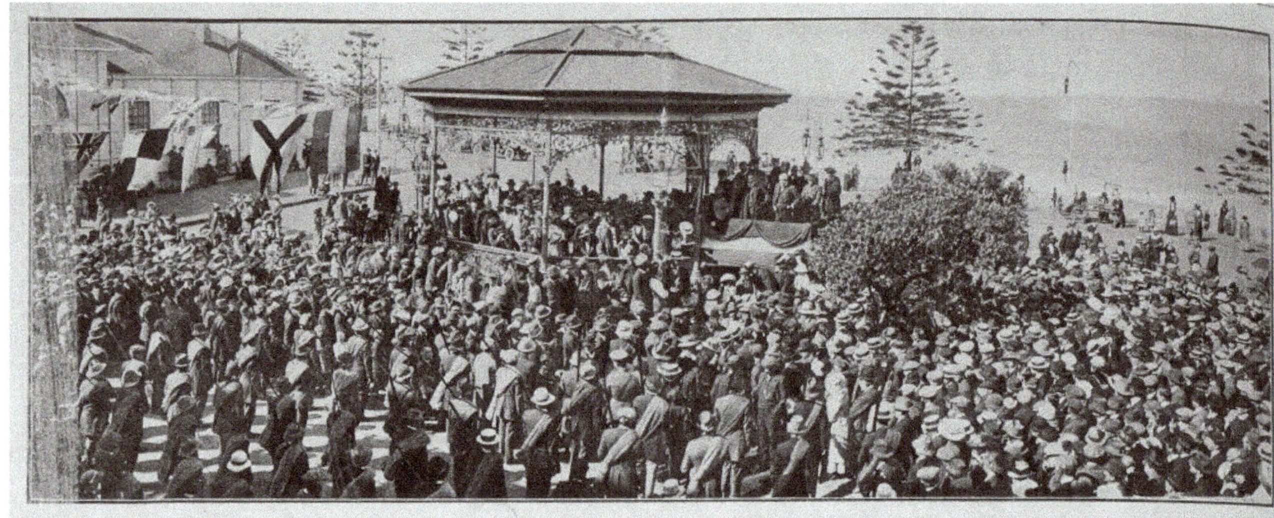

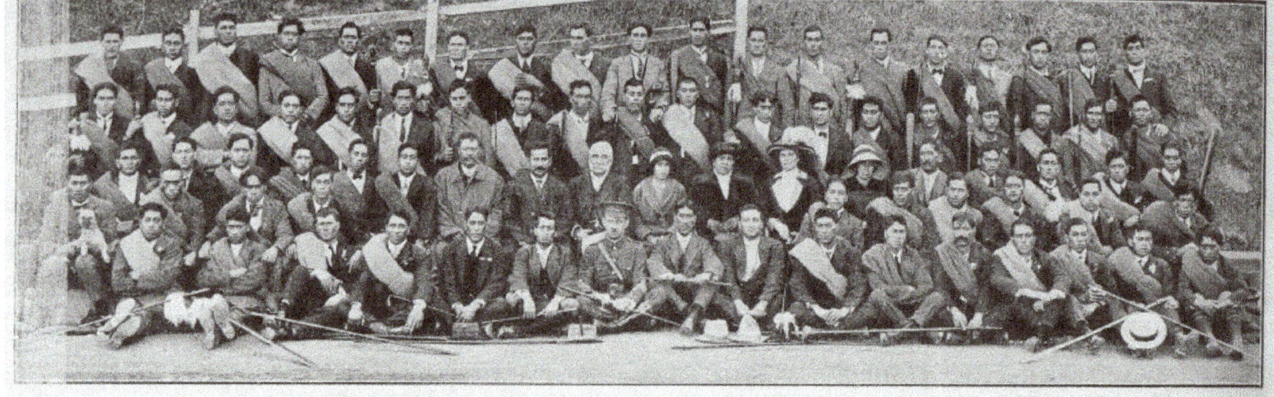

The above photo is a group portrait of the East Coast section of the Maori Expeditionary Force for service abroad, and others. In the centre of the front row is Mr John Vigor Brown, M.P., Mayor of Napier and at his right hand is the Hon. Apirana Turupa Ngata, M.P. [53]

---

[52] No known Copyright. From the 'Sir George Grey Special Collections, Auckland Libraries, AWNS-19141029-46-1.' Taken from the supplement to the Auckland Weekly News, 29 October 1914, p46

[53] No known Copyright. From the 'Sir George Grey Special Collections, Auckland Libraries, AWNS-19141029-46-2'

On 3 August 1942, the railway line north of Napier to Gisborne opened. These photos show two engines drawing a heavy freight train up the Kopuawhara rise, the first day the line was in use, and also the 219 metres long Waipaoa bridge, near Gisborne, crossing the Waipaoa River. [54]

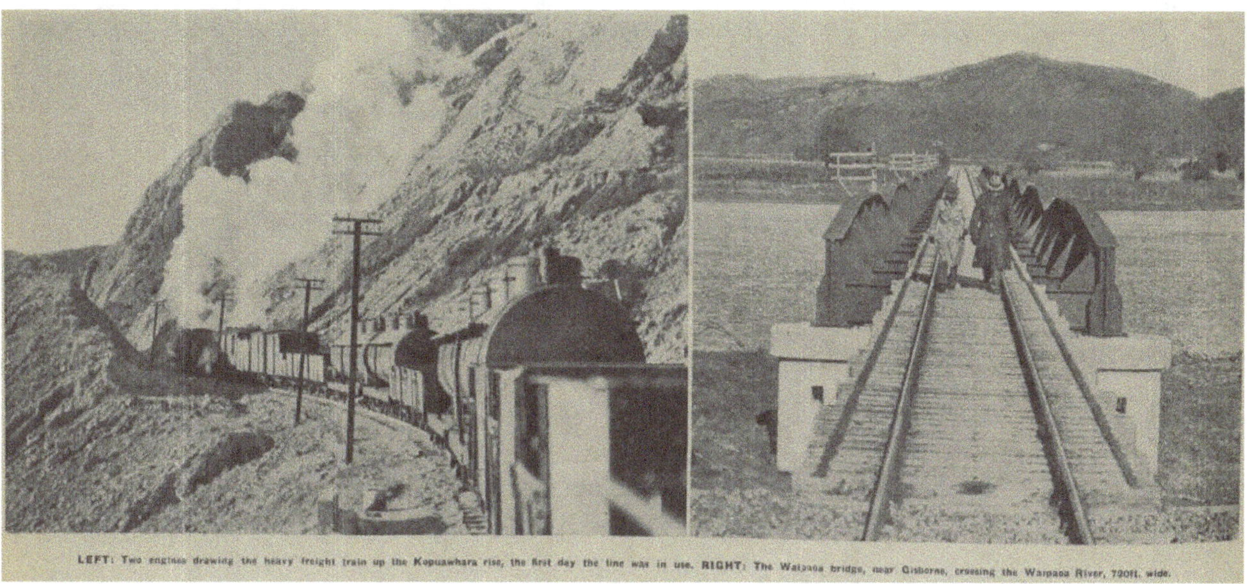

In September of 1942 passenger services began. [55]

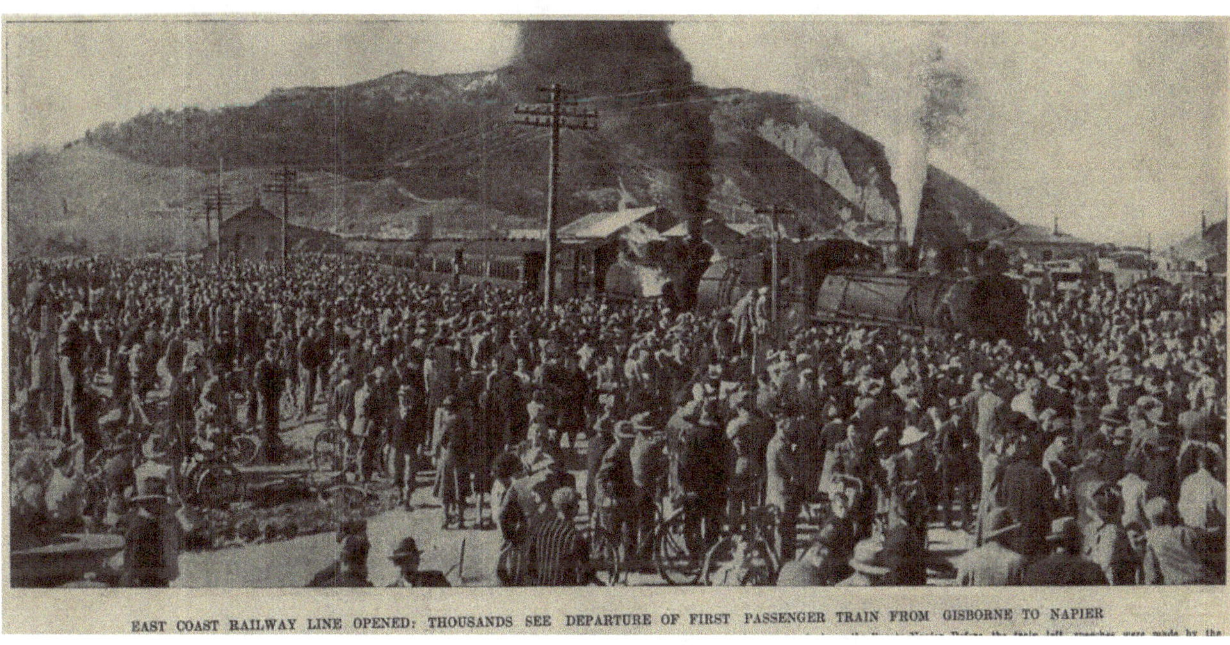

---

[54] No known Copyright. From the 'Sir George Grey Special Collection, Auckland Libraries, AWNS-19420812-14-3.' Taken from the supplement to the Auckland Weekly News 12 August 1942 p14.

[55] No known Copyright. From 'Sir George Grey Special Collections, Auckland Libraries, Auckland Weekly New. AWNS-19420916-20-3'

1	2	3	4
5	6	7	8
9	10	11	12
13	14	15	16
17	18	19	20
21	22	23	24
25	26	27	28
29	30	31	

September

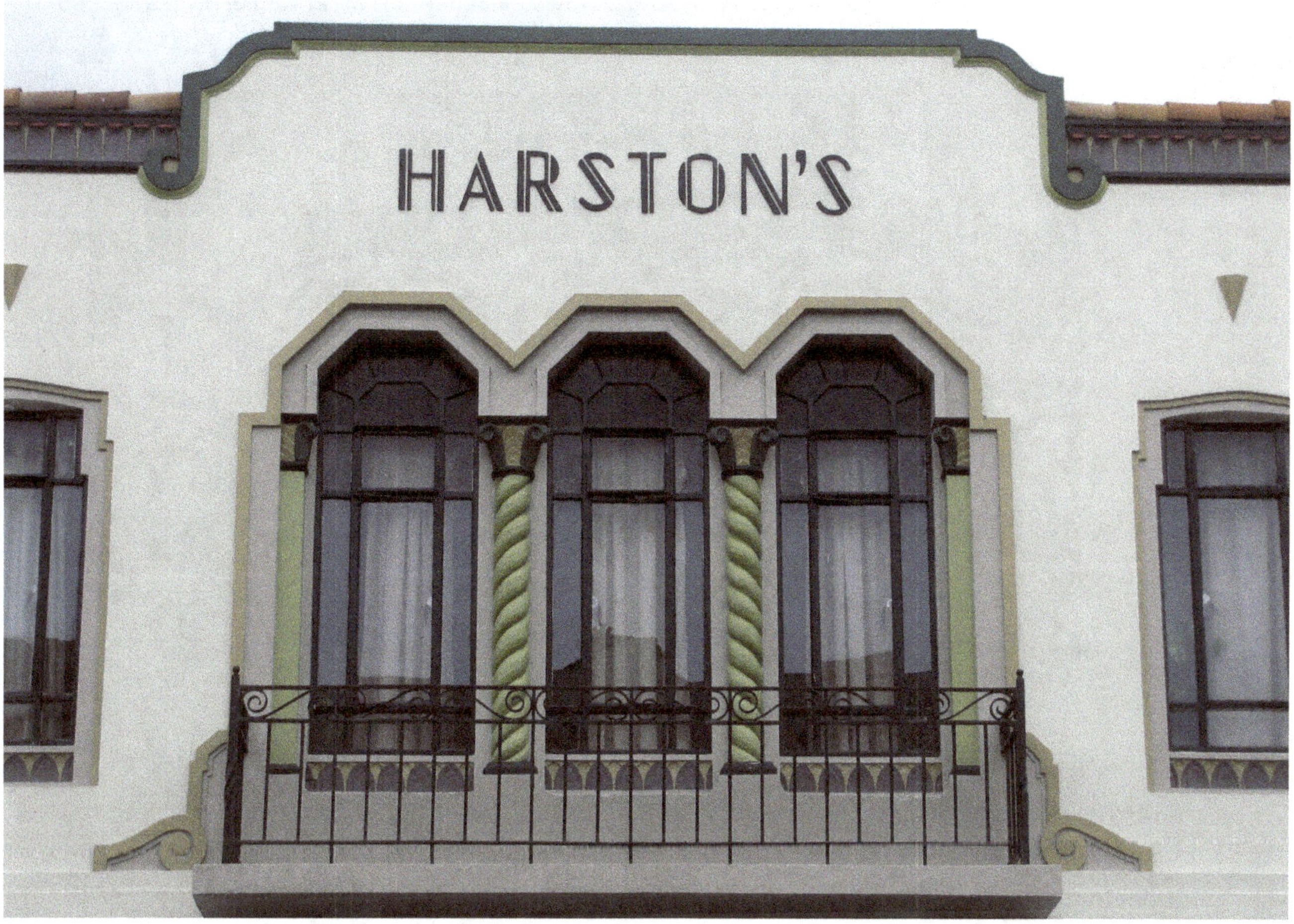

The Harston's building was reinstated in 1932 after the earthquake after being extensively damaged as shown in the photograph below. The architect was EA Williams in Napier, and the builder was WM Angus Ltd. The style is described as Spanish Mission. The Harston's music store, owned by Neville Harston, was a popular shop in Napier from 1930 until 1986.

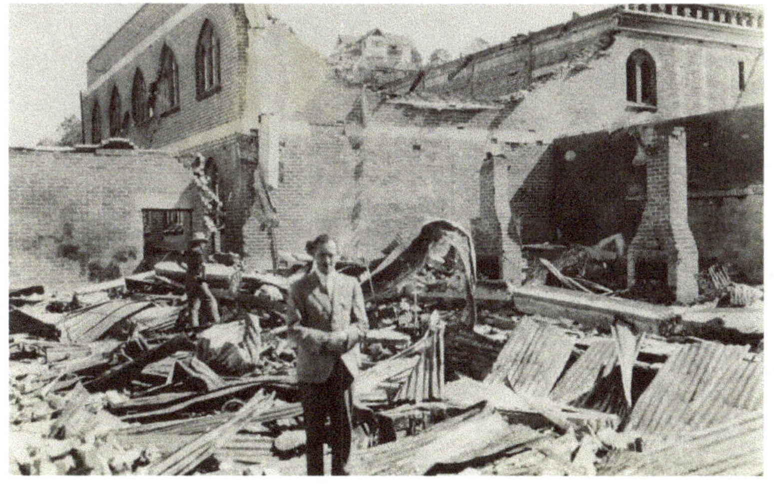

A photograph from the Citizens of Napier Archive: "The proprietor's son, Neville Harston, surveys the ruins of Harston's Music Warehouse after the devastation of the 1931 Napier Earthquake".[56]

[56] © Citizens of Napier Archive (with grateful thanks to Dr M.N.D. Campbell and family). Provided by Christopher Matthews Photographer

Memorable events in September:

On 7 September 1921, the Springboks played the New Zealand Maori XV at Napier. The Springboks won 9-8

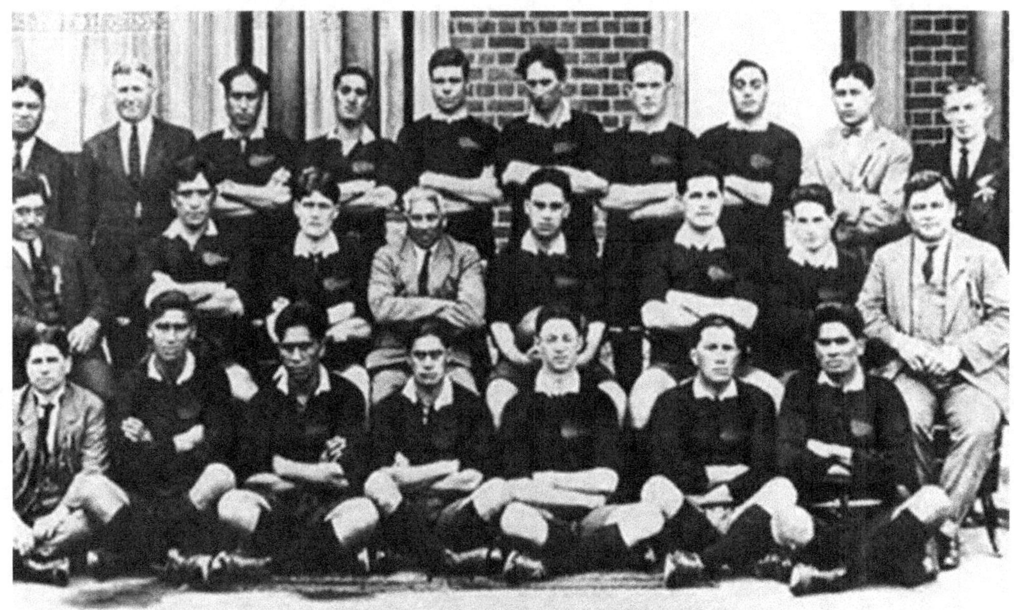

The 1921 New Zealand Maori Team

The New Zealand Maori team was captained by Parekura Tureia (Ngati Porou) and managed by Ned Parata (Ngai Tahu). The team list printed in a newspaper at the time was: Full-back: T. Kuru; Three-quarters: J. Blake, Barclay, Tapsell; Five-eighths: Tureia and Peina; Half- back: Mill; Rover, Jacobs; Forwards: Mitai, Kororiko, B. Gemmell, Grace, Garlick, Broughton, Te Whata. Reserves: Edwards, M. Blake, Tangitu, Carroll, and Ormond.

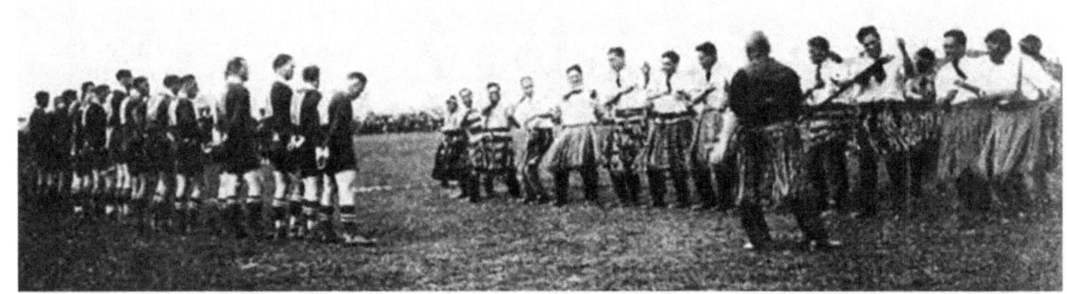

The New Zealand Maori team performs a haka before the game

---

[57] Photos – Courtesy of the New Zealand Rugby Museum

In 1968 Napier celebrated the opening of the Civic Administration Centre in the Civic Block bounded by Station, Vautier and Hastings Streets.

The previous borough council building located at Tennyson Street and Herschell Streets was relocated to Byron Street and is now used as a community arts facility.

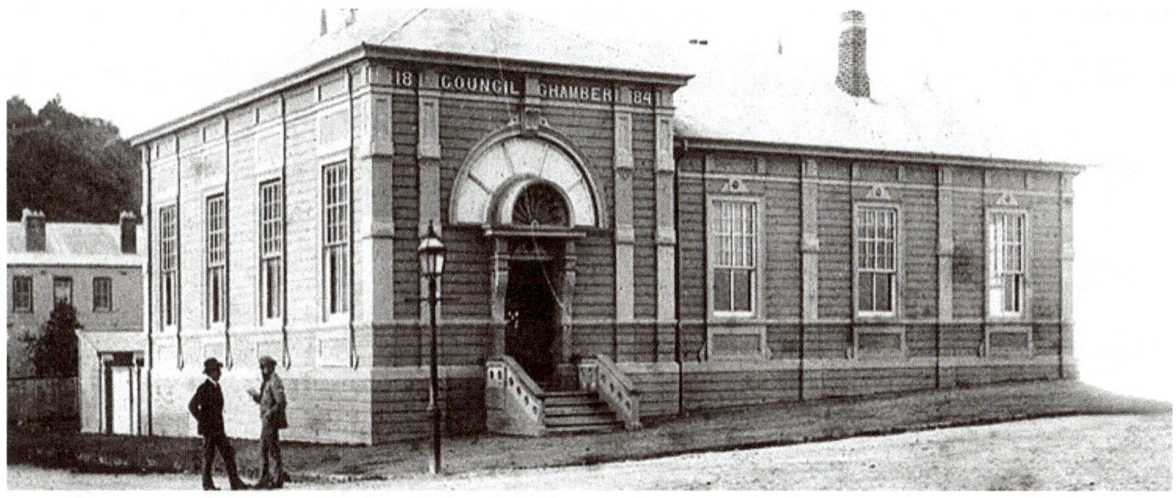

The first Napier Borough Council was elected in 1875. The Council was initially located in the former Provincial Council offices but moved to the new Borough Council Chambers constructed in 1884. This was one of the few buildings from the prior century to survive the 1931 earthquake.

On 9 September 2005, British American Tobacco announced it would close the Rothmans factory in Napier, due to reduced demand, resulting in a loss of about 170 jobs locally.

Thomas Murray, who was chief officer of the s.s. Wonga Wonga on her first visit to Napier, became pilot and harbourmaster in September 1858, his salary being £100 a year[58].

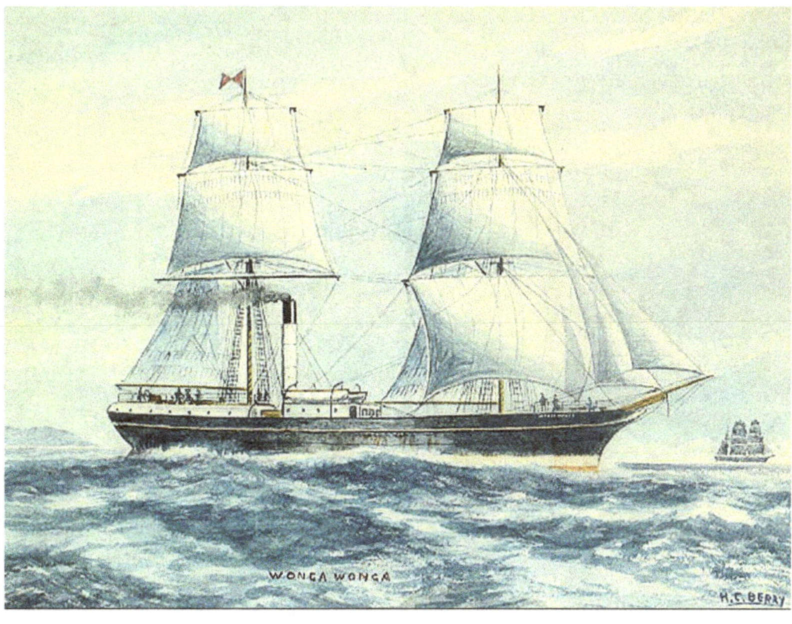

---

[58] Source: White Wings Vol. II. Founding of the Provinces and Old-Time Shipping. Passenger Ships from 1840 to 1885. Chapter VII – Port of Napier. Author: Henry Brett. 1928, Part of: New Zealand Texts Collection. License: Creative Commons Attribution-Share Alike 3.0 New Zealand Licence

The original Ahuriri harbour in the 1850s was difficult to use and navigate, particularly at the channel entry as can be seen in this early painting by Joseph Rhodes[59]

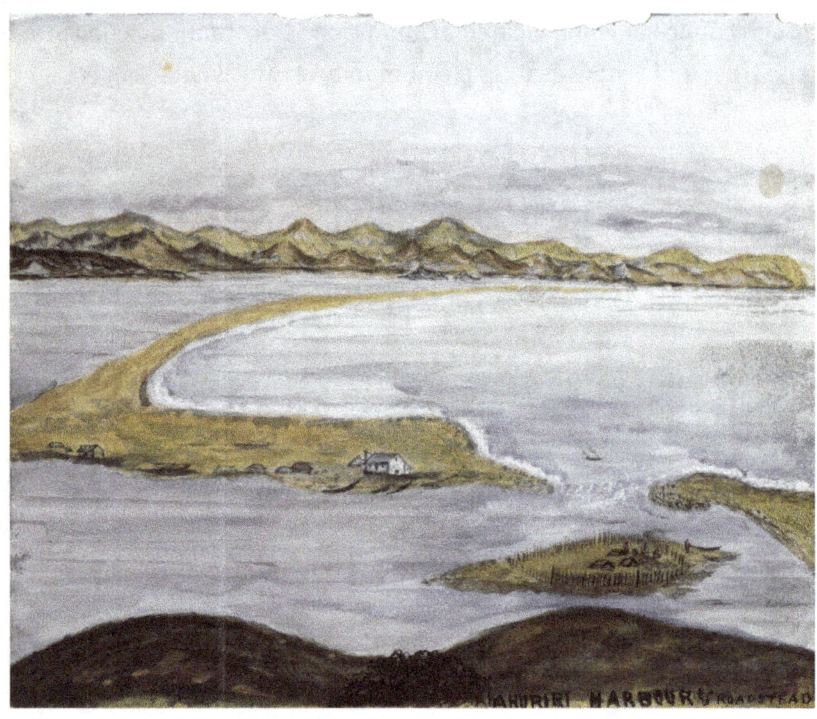

Over the following years the harbour developed with the increase in trade as in this photo[60] circa 1886, but it was not until 1886 that the Breakwater Harbour was completed, and the Breakwater wharf in 1893. In 1895 the timber constructed Glasgow Wharf was opened.

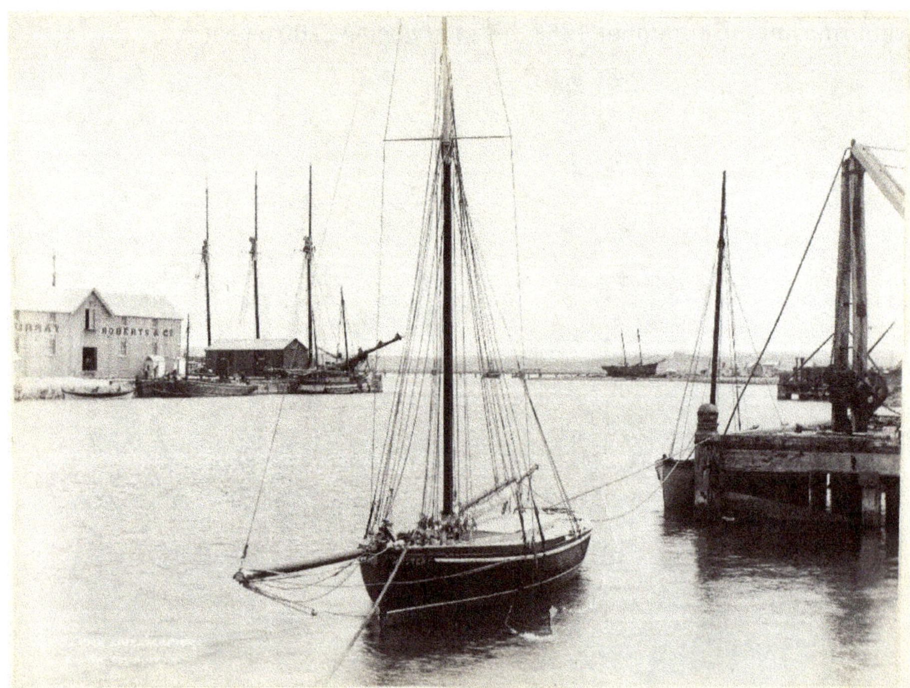

---

[59] Ahuriri harbour and homestead. Alexander Turnbull Library, Wellington. Reference: A-159-033. Artist: Joseph Rhodes, 1826-1905.

[60] Source: Collection of Museum of New Zealand, Te Papa. Photo by Burton Brothers studio, 1880s, Dunedin. Public domain.

1	2	3	4
5	6	7	8
9	10	11	12
13	14	15	16
17	18	19	20
21	22	23	24
25	26	27	28
29	30		

October

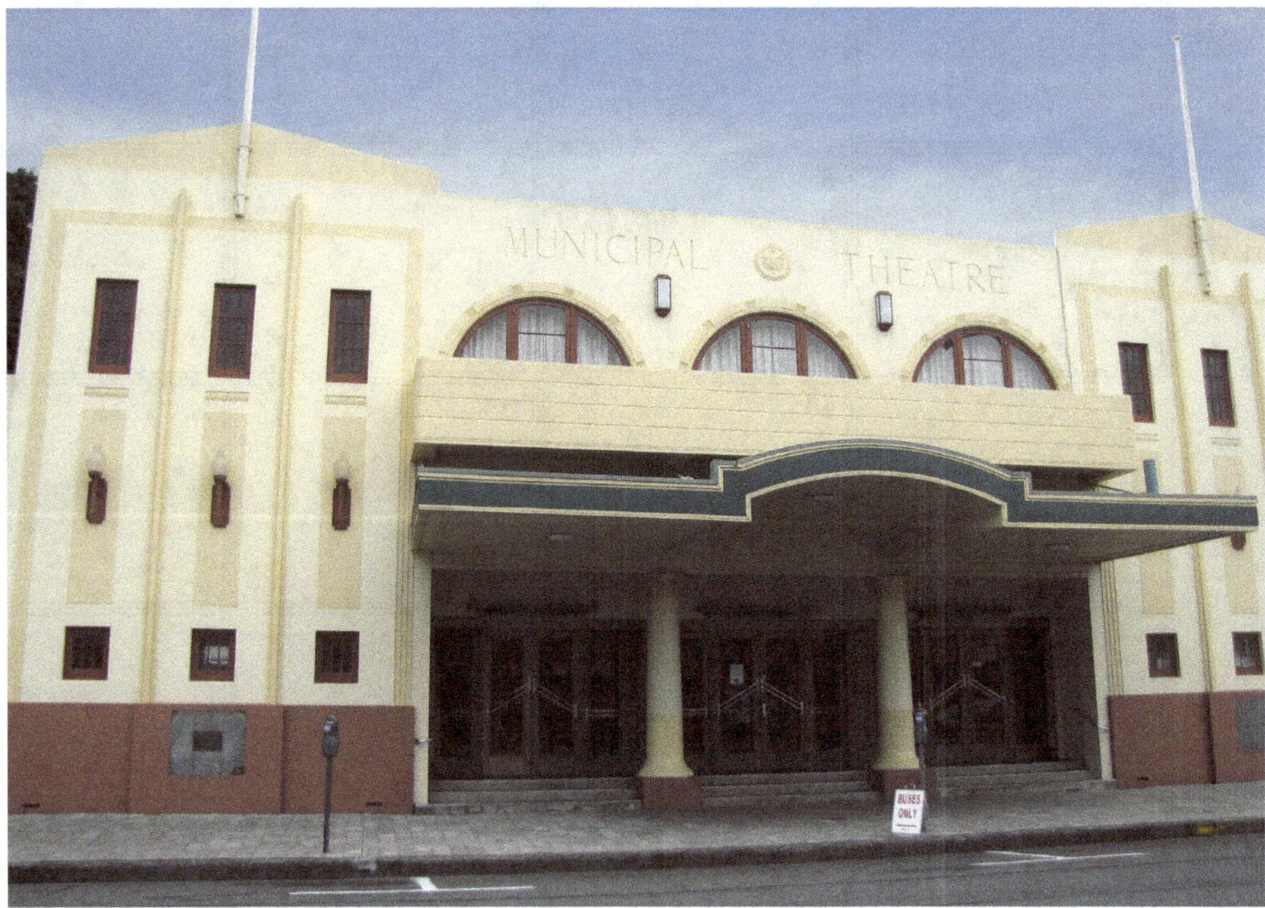

The original theatre building was built in 1912, and designed by William Pitt. The new building was designed by the architectural firm JT Watson in Napier. It was built by WM Angus Ltd and was finished in 1937. Its style is Art Deco. There have been various additions and alterations to the present day.

Memorable events in October:

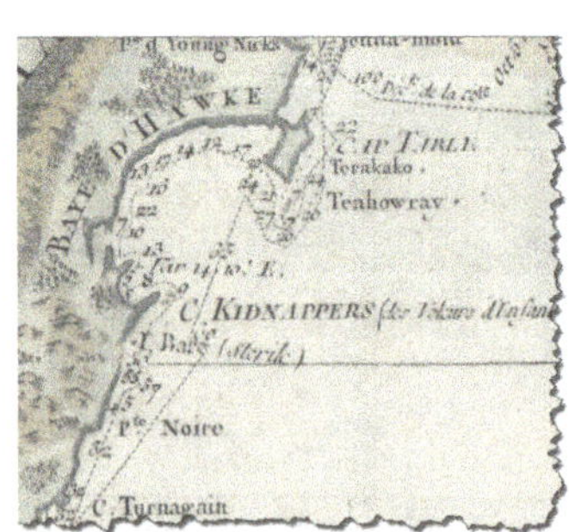

On 14 October 1769, Captain James Cook's ship 'Endeavour' stood off the Napier bluff. Cook named the Bay in honour of Sir Edward Hawke, First Lord of the Admiralty.

The Napier Harbour Board was formed on 21 October 1875. The port was moved from the Ahuriri spit to its current location, when the initial breakwater was completed in 1886.

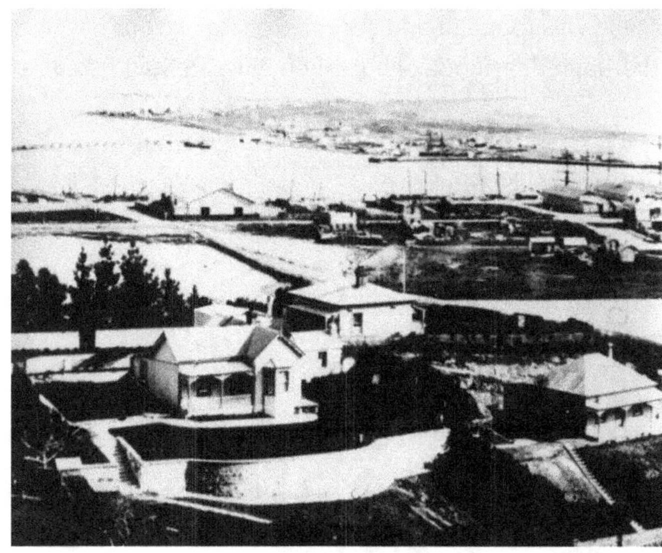

The port in 1868[61]

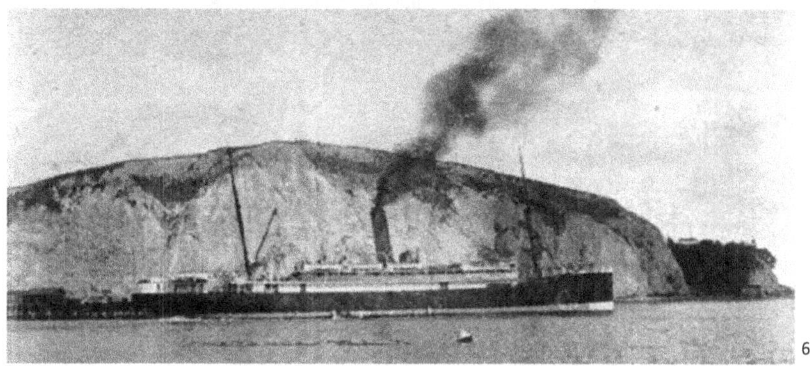

The S.S. Manuel at Glasgow wharf

The port wharves suffered considerable damage in the 1931 earthquake [63]

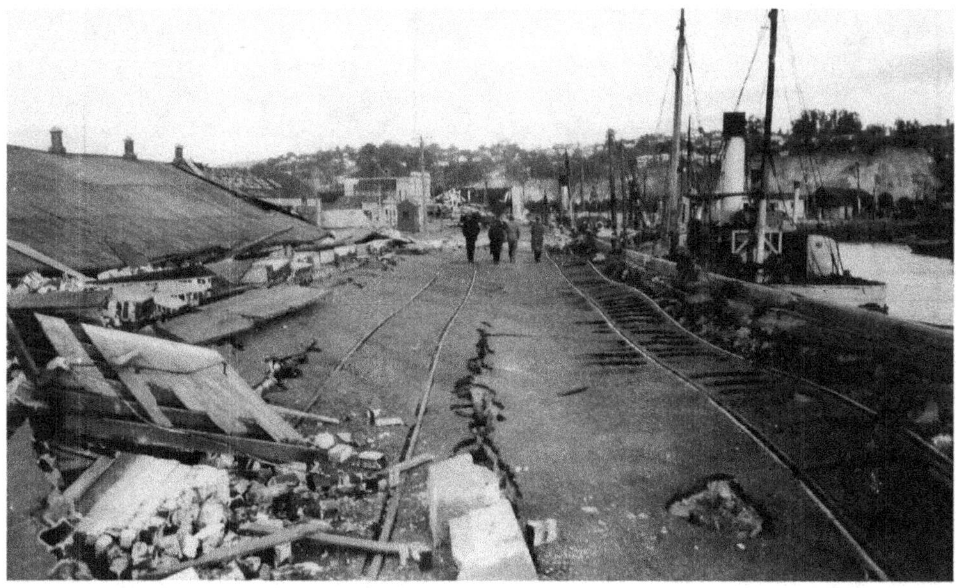

In October 1876, the Napier Volunteer Fire Brigade was founded and occupied a site in front of the Masonic Hotel. The building was damaged in the Napier earthquake but when it was rebuilt it kept a similar façade.

In October 1858 the first bank, Union Bank of Australia opened.

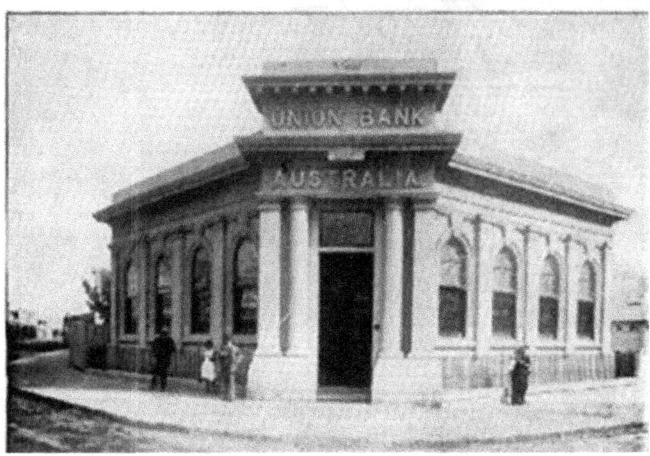

In the month of October in 1954 the East Coast Farmers' Fertilizer Company began production at Awatoto.

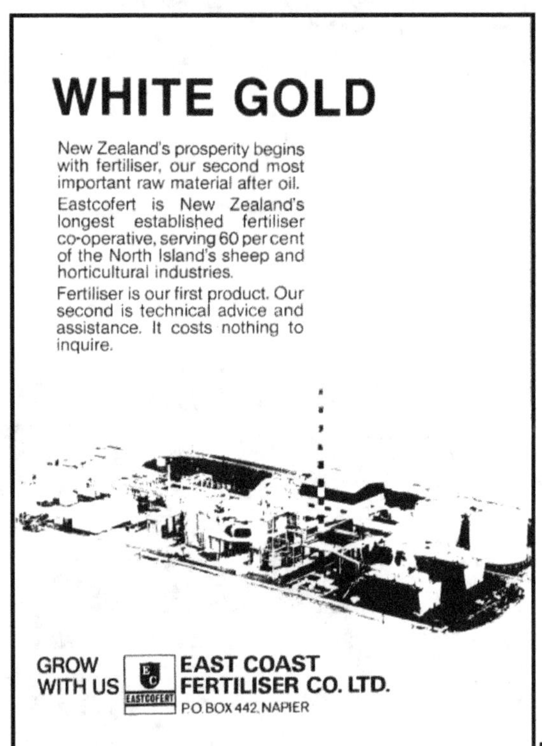

Early advertisement by Eastcofert

In 1979 East Coast Framers Fertiliser celebrated 25 years of production. The company merged with Ravensdown Fertiliser in 1987.

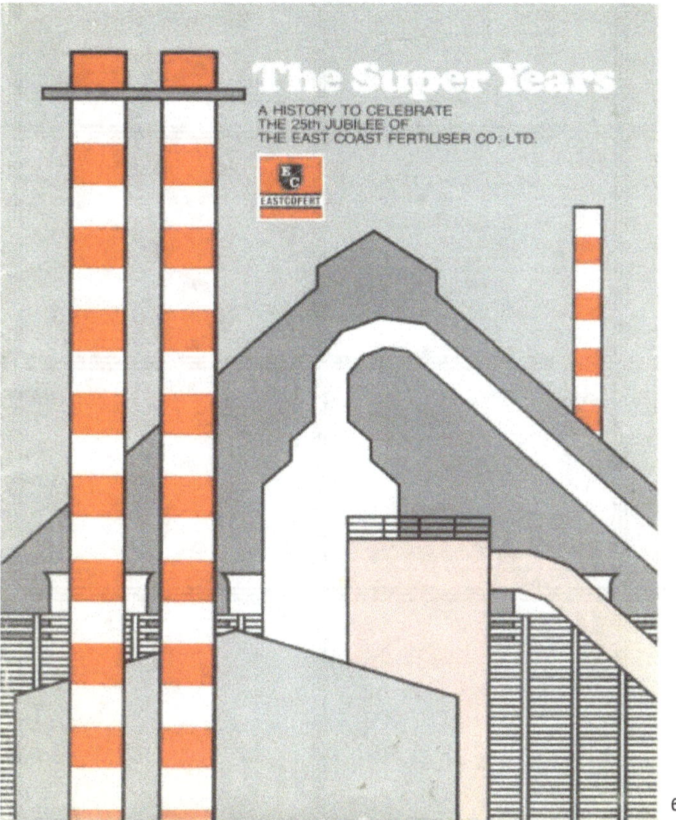

64

The last scheduled steam train service from Napier to Gisborne left on 7 October 1966.[65]

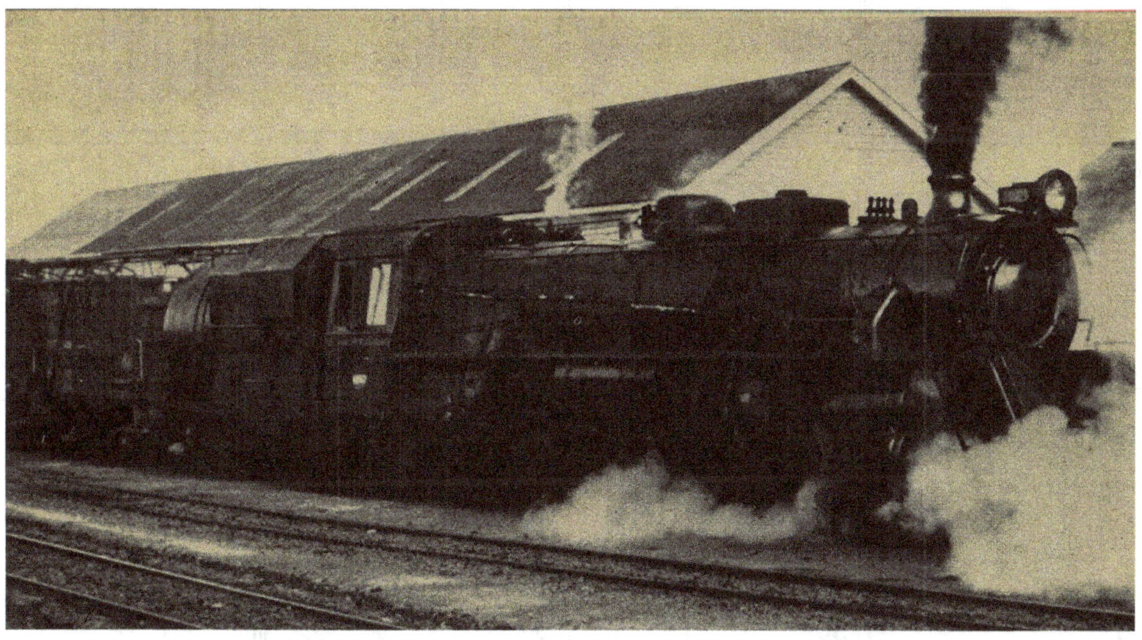

---

[64] Front cover image of "The Super Years" booklet. Author Kate Contos Publisher: East Coast Fertiliser Co. Ltd, Year published: 1979. Used with permission by Knowledge Bank - HB Digital Archives Trust www.knowledgebank.org.nz

[65] HB Photo News image. Used with permission by Knowledge Bank - HB Digital Archives Trust www.knowledgebank.org.nz

1	2	3	4
5	6	7	8
9	10	11	12
13	14	15	16
17	18	19	20
21	22	23	24
25	26	27	28
29	30	31	

November

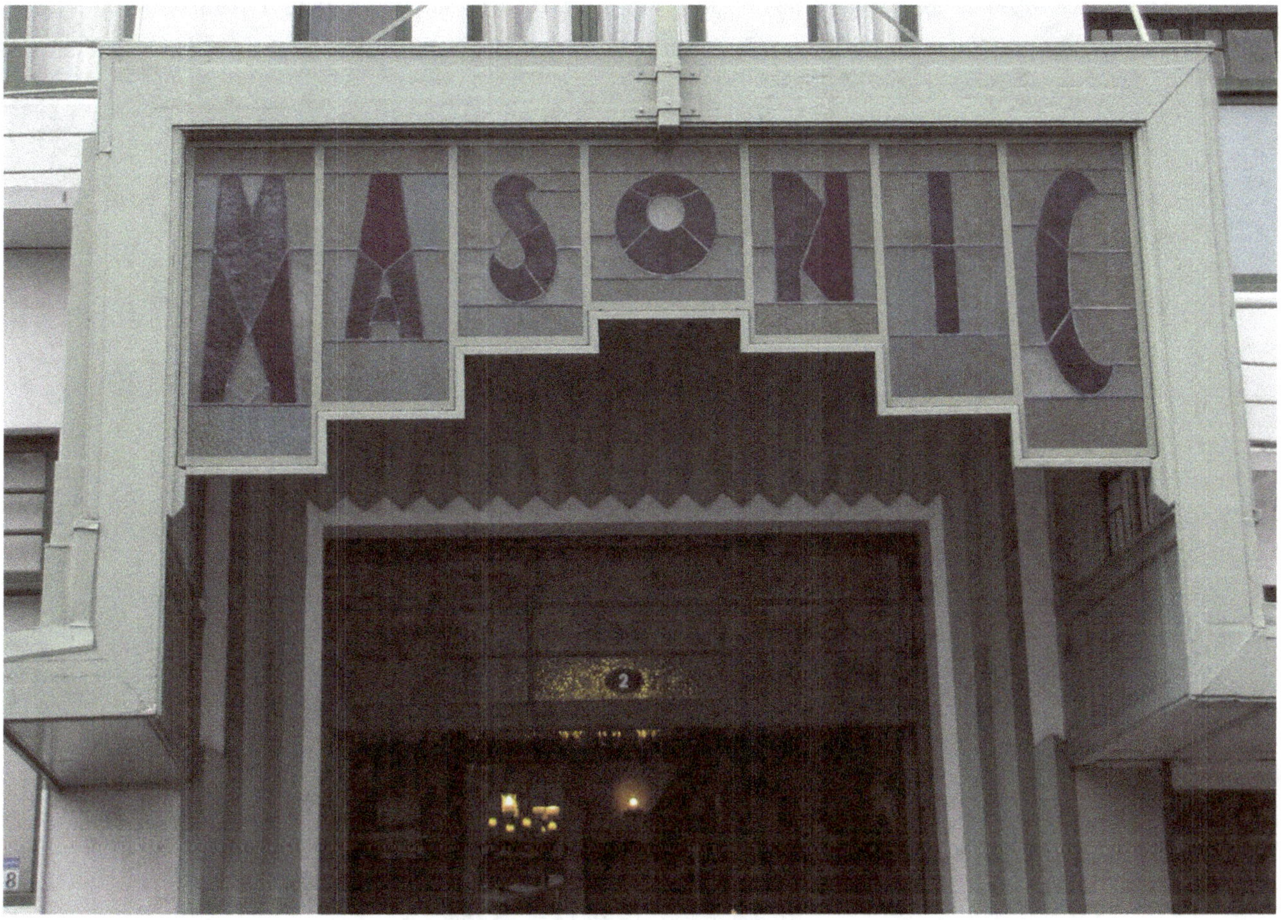

The architectural firm for the Masonic building was Prouse & Wilson and it was designed by Norman Wilson. The building was constructed by Edwards Construction Company, and it was finished in 1932. The style of the building is Art Deco. The original owner was John Vigor Brown and it was used as a hotel and for shops. Queen Elizabeth II stayed at the Masonic during her 1953-54 Royal tour.

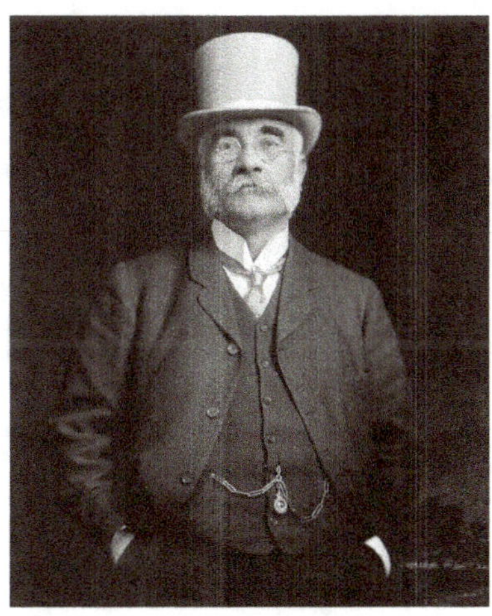

John Vigor Brown was mayor of Napier at the time of the 1931 earthquake (at the age of 76) and much credit is owed to him for his legacy of hard work and a vision for post-earthquake Napier. He also served as a MP for Napier from 1908 to 1922.

Memorable events in November:

On 1 November 1858, Hawke's Bay was declared a province of New Zealand. On 29 November 1874 Napier was proclaimed a borough. The town was divided into five districts with a total of 493 electors.

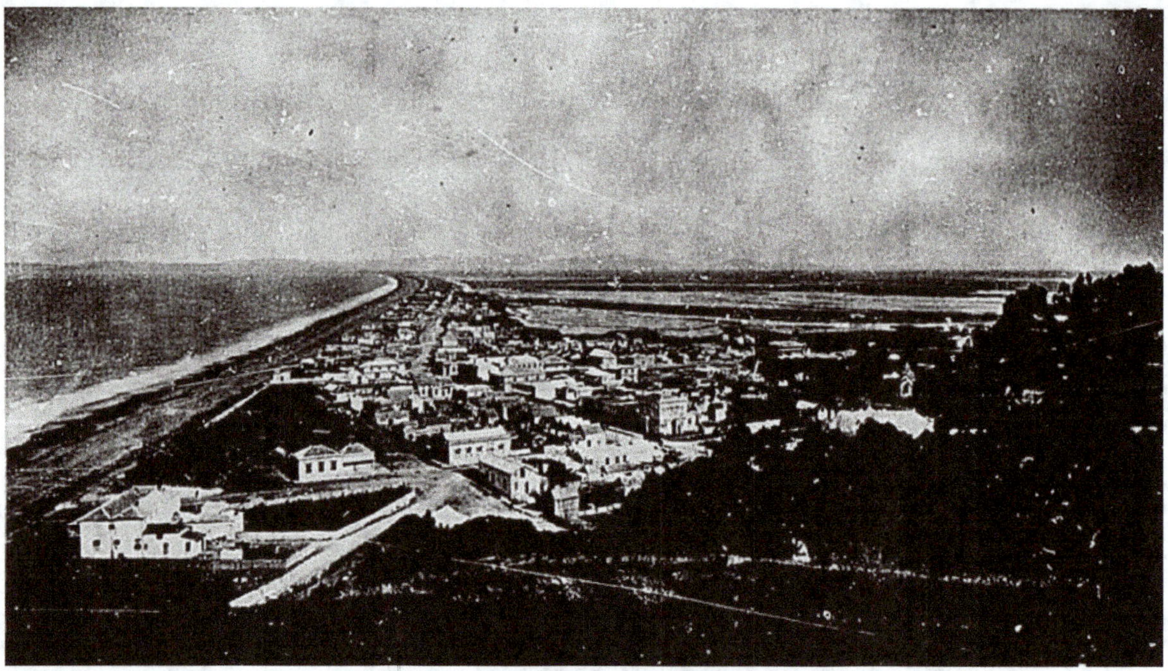

Napier in 1875 [66]

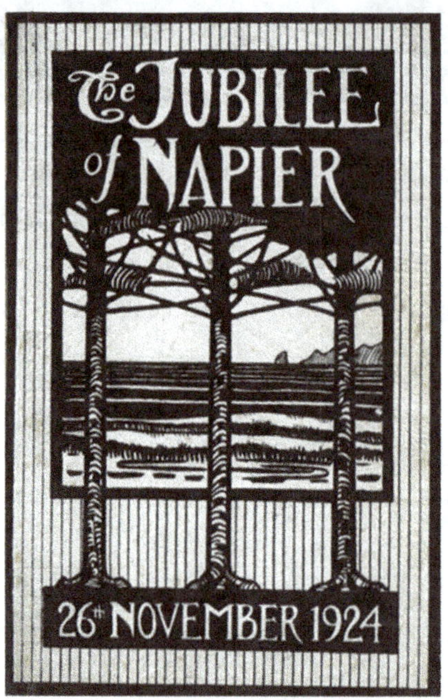

[67]

The 50th jubilee of Napier was celebrated in November 1924.

In November 1870 construction began on the Napier- Taradale Road which included three miles of roadway and two bridges (one across the tidal lagoon at Burton's Gully and the other across the Tutaekuri River). There was major damage to the Napier-Taradale road in the 1931 earthquake.

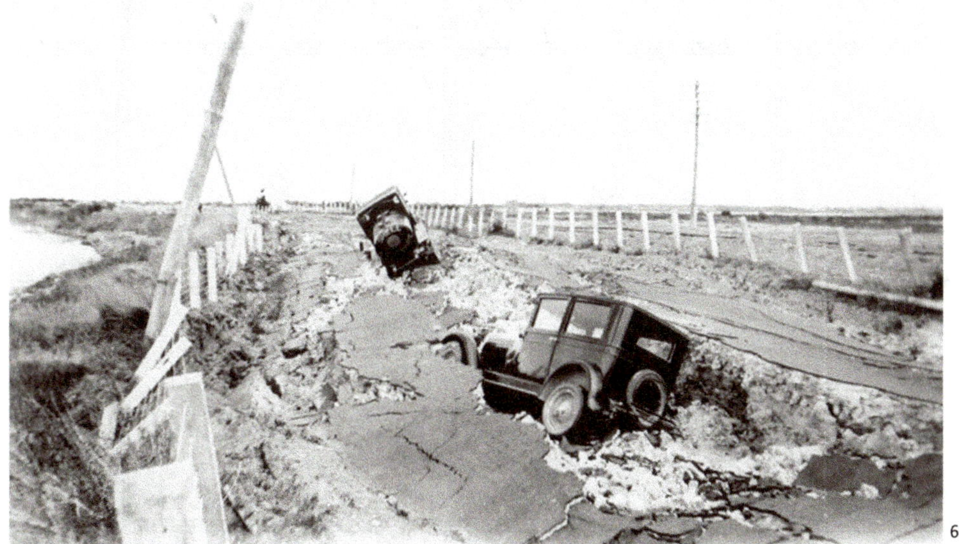

Tolls originally levied to repay the costs of construction and maintenance were withdrawn in 1875 due to the popularity of the road. The road was extensively damaged in the 1931 earthquake.

This crossing over the Tutaekuri River was a considerable improvement on the old method in the 1800s as can be seen in this very old photo:[69]

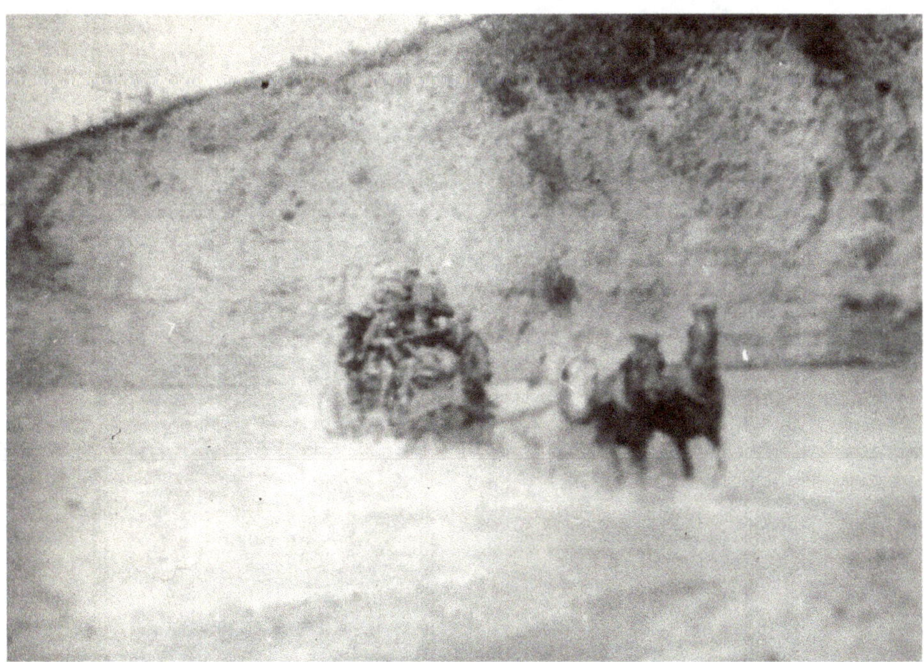

---

[68] "Taradale Road, Napier," F Furkert (b.1876, d.1949), photographer, collection of Hawke's Bay Museums Trust, Ruawharo Tā-ū-rangi, 15791.

[69] Crossing the Tutaekuri river. Photo from RD 9 Historical Trust collection. Used with permission by Knowledge Bank - HB Digital Archives Trust www.knowledgebank.org.nz

1	2	3	4
5	6	7	8
9	10	11	12
13	14	15	16
17	18	19	20
21	22	23	24
25	26	27	28
29	30		

December

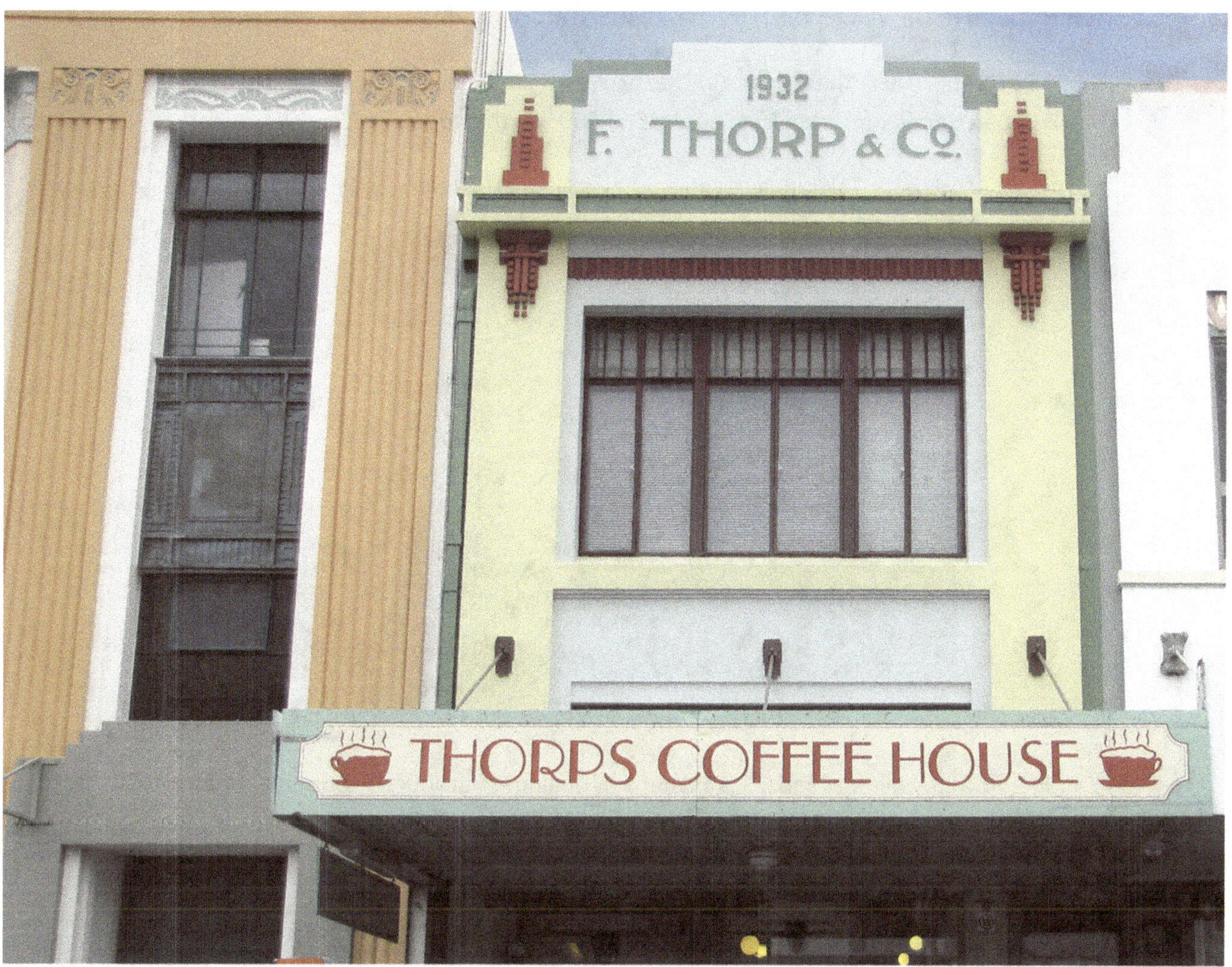

The Thorps Coffee House building was constructed in 1932. The architect was JA Louis Hay and it was built by the Fletcher Construction Company. The style of the building is described as Art Deco with FL Wright influences. F. Thorp was originally a shoe merchant and the coffee shop opened when the shoe shop closed in the early 1900s.

Final Clearance Sale

FOR FOURTEEN DAYS,

FOR CASH ONLY.

OWING to our New Shipments arriving, we must Reduce our Immense Stocks of BOOTS, SHOES, and SLIPPERS, comprising all the latest Styles of ENGLISH, AMERICAN, and COLONIAL MANUFACTURES. The following Prices speak for themselves, including all the well-known GOOD BRANDS :—

SPECIMEN LIST—

	Sale Price. s. d.	Usual Price. s. d.
Gent's Calf Sewn COOKHAMS, Wide Welts	14 6	20 0
Gent's English Goloshed Sewn BALMORALS, New Line.	6 11	10 6
Gent's English Calf Goloshed Sewn BALMORALS, Kid Leg	11 6	15 6
Men's Kip Pegged WATERTIGHTS, Grand Value	7 11	11 6
Men's Kip Nailed SHOOTEES, Solid Wear	7 11	11 6
Men's Hand-sewn Porpoise COOKHAMS	20 0	32 6
Ladies' Satin Calf Sewn SHOES, New Goods	5 11	8 6
Ladies' Tan Cross and Instep Strap SHOES.	7 11	12 6
Ladies' Glace SHOES, Pollak's, Stylish Wear	6 6	12 6

And an endless variety of Boys' and Girls' Boots, Shoes, and Slippers at the same Reductions.

NO SALE GOODS BOOKED OR SENT ON APPROVAL.
Country Orders, Accompanied with Cash, will receive Prompt Attention.
NOTE THE ADDRESS and Call upon your Old Friends, and you will receive Complete Satisfaction.

R. Thorp. and Co.,

(LATE F. WILSON AND CO.)
HASTINGS STREET, NAPIER, AND AT HASTINGS.

Ring Up Telephone No. 230.   P.O. Box 74.

Advertisement from the Daily Telegraph, 1 October 1897.

Memorable events in December

In the month of December 1884, the new council offices and town hall were ready for occupation.

On 18 December 1886, the "Great Fire" destroyed 26 buildings among them the Daily Telegraph and Hawke's Bay Herald offices causing nearly £60,000 worth of damage.

In December 1912 s.s. Takapuna began a wharf-to- wharf passenger service between Gisborne and Napier.

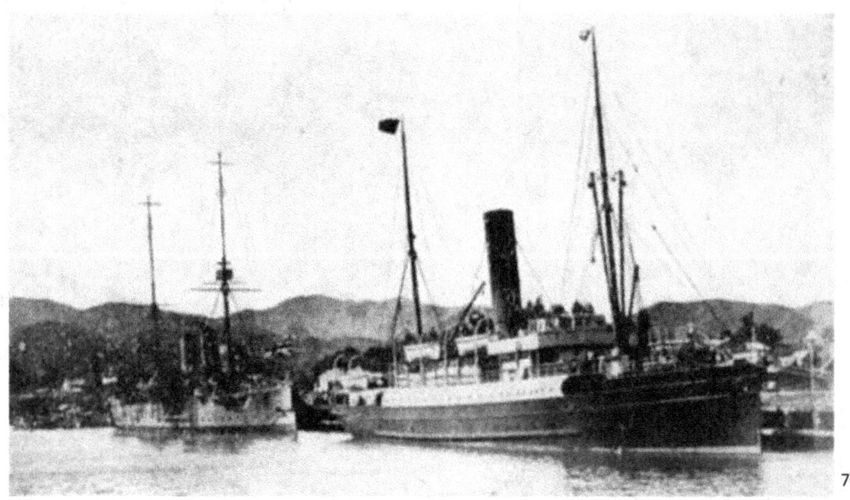

H.M.S. Philomel and S.S. Takapuna in old inner harbour, Gisborne, February 1914

In December 1932, the Masonic Hotel opened for bar trade.

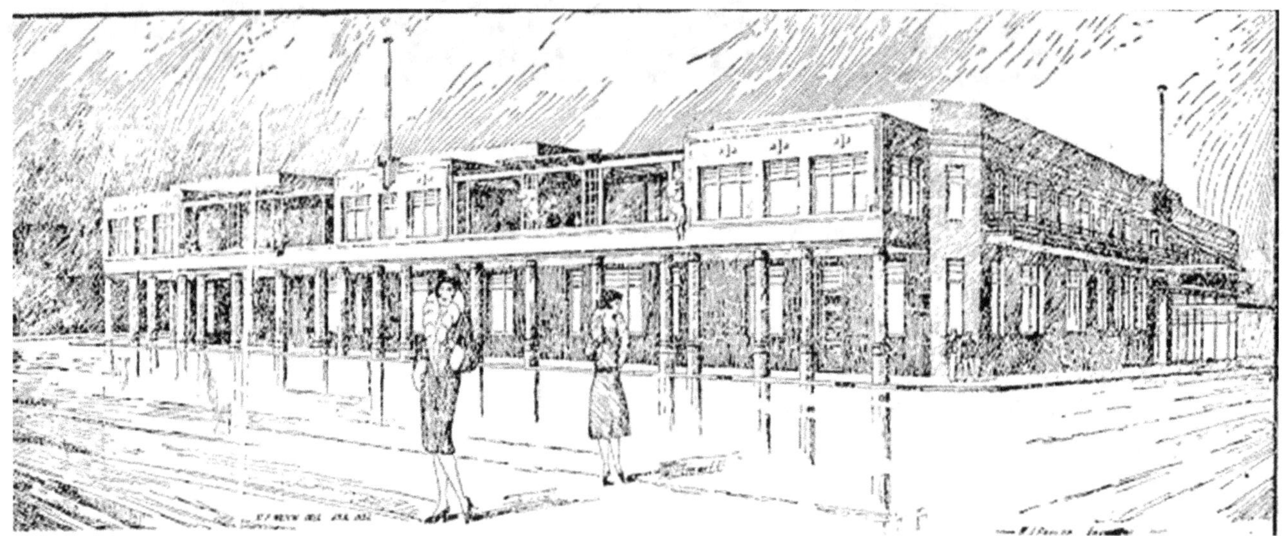

Image from the Auckland Star 14 April, 1932. The article announced the contract for the reconstruction of the Masonic Hotel for the sum of £40,000. The illustration is the front profile of the building by the architect Mr W Prouse of Wellington.[71]

---

[70] "H.M.S. Philomel" by Joseph Angus Mackay, The New Zealand Electronic Text Collection (CC BY-SA).

[71] Illustration reproduced with the permission of Fairfax Media and the successor architectural firm to Gummer and Ford (Ministry of Architecture + Interiors – MOAI).

The first Fokker Friendship aircraft landed on the new sealed 1310 m runway at the airport in 1963.

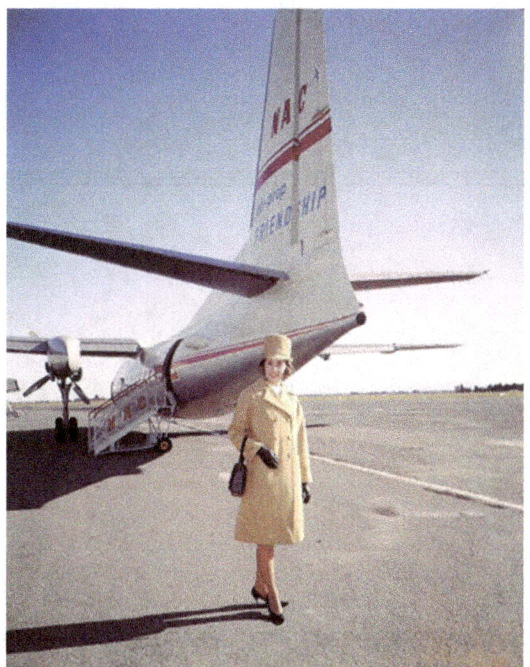

NAC stewardess and Fokker Friendship

Fokker Friendship at Napier Airport, Xmas Day 1964[73]

---

[72] "Air Hostess Uniform 1965 Gold" by Archives New Zealand, FLICKR (CC BY-SA).

[73] Photo by F. Pomeroy. Used with permission by Knowledge Bank - HB Digital Archives Trust www.knowledgebank.org.nz

1	2	3	4
5	6	7	8
9	10	11	12
13	14	15	16
17	18	19	20
21	22	23	24
25	26	27	28
29	30	31	

Art Deco in Napier

The term Art Deco was coined in the 1960s. Today it is used to describe the many variations of the style that evolved from around 1905, and in particular after the 1925 *"Exposition des Arts Decoratifs et Industriels"* in Paris.

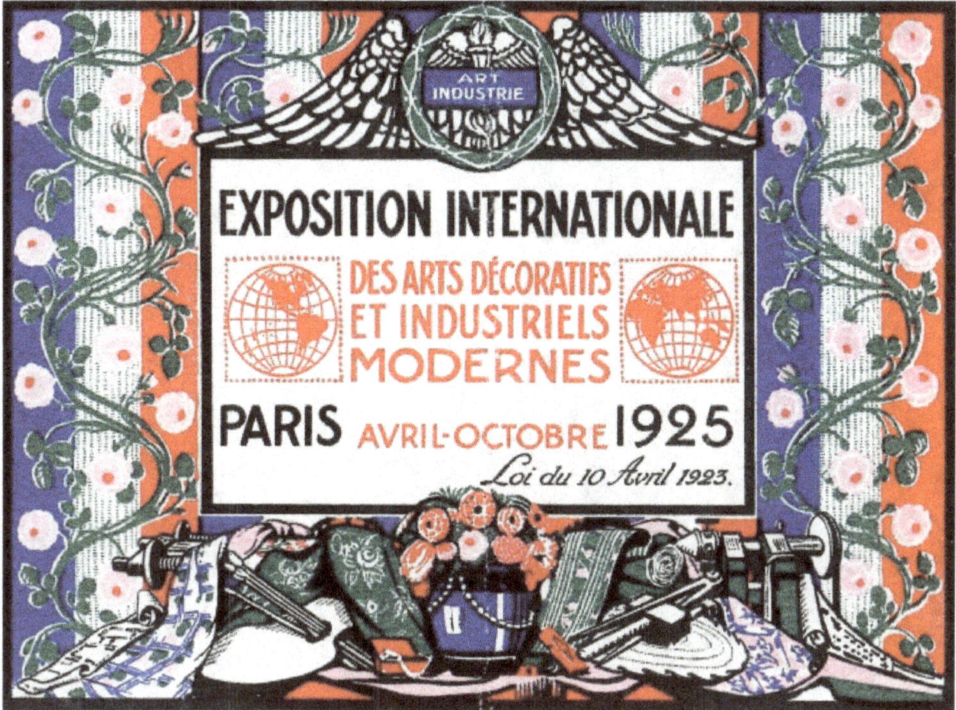

The style progressed from its early classical influence that was evident at the Paris exposition such as in the following building[74] for Galeries Lafayette (a large French department store chain):

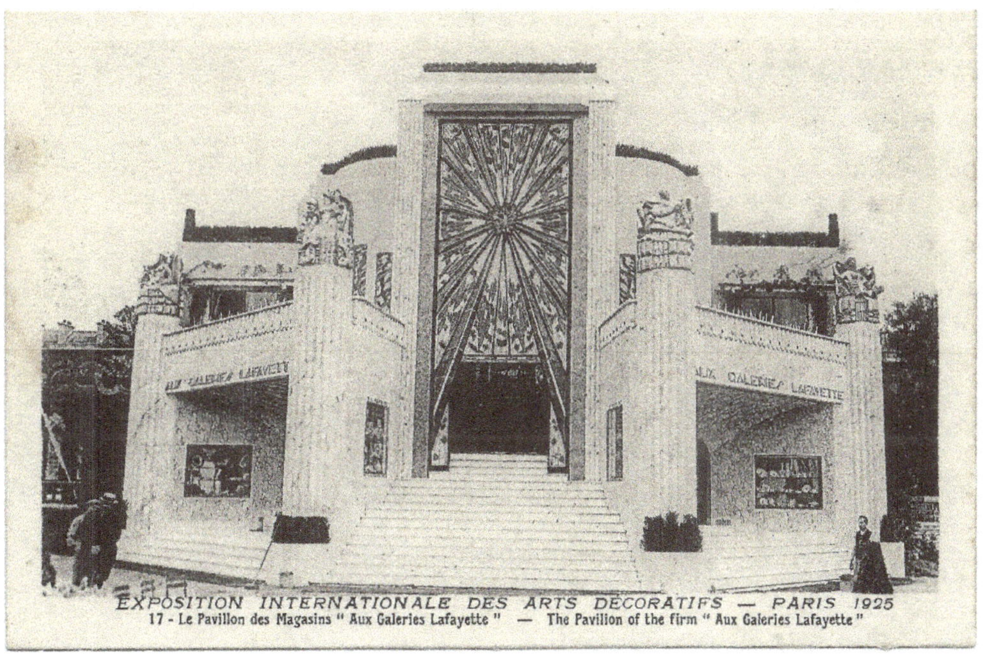

---

[74] Source : Wikimedia. Carte postale - éditeur : Les Éditions artistiques LIP : Paris & ses Merveilles - imprimeur : J. Cormault à Paris

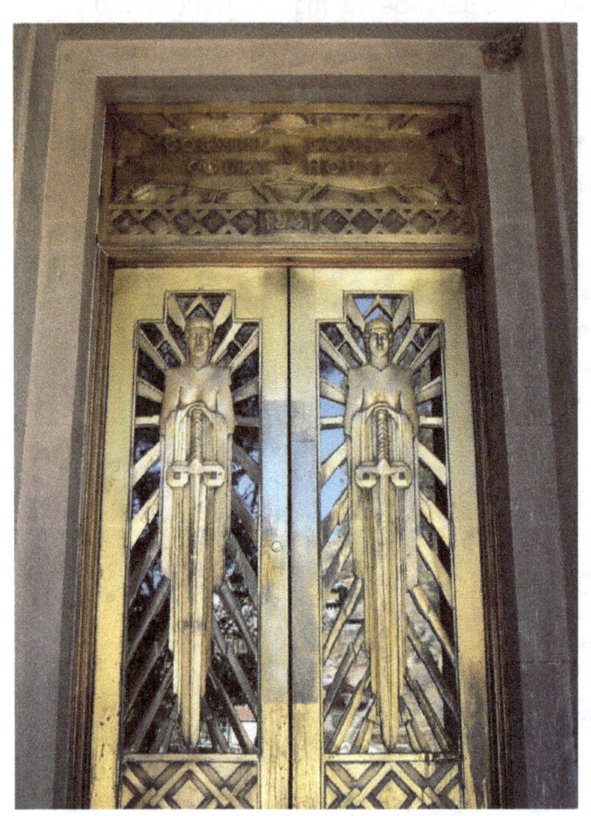

Then the style developed with an Egyptian influenced stage in the late twenties (with its "zig-zag" features) such as in the door to this courthouse in the USA[75]

After that, the art deco style developed into a more streamlined "moderne" style in the 1930s, such as can be seen in the San Francisco Maritime Museum building of 1936.[76]

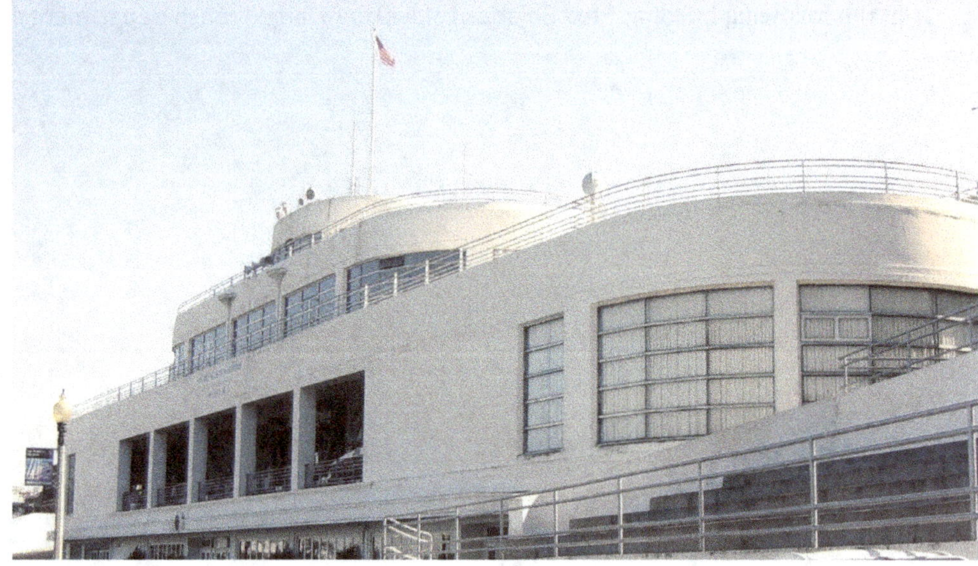

[75] Photo by Peter Bronski, 2010. Source Wikipedia.

[76] Photo by Leonard G. (CC by SA)

Art Deco Styles

The foreword to the Napier City Council Art Deco Inventory [77] written by the late Robert McGregor, the then Executive Director of the Art Deco Trust, provides an excellent analysis and summary of the different art deco styles used in Napier. The "Signage Guidelines" leaflet produced by Napier City Council Planning Department in May 2009 also incorporates some helpful descriptions and explanations. This part of the book incorporates some of this material.

The Signage Guidelines leaflet outlines:

"...The clean lines, streamlining and symmetry of Art Deco designs reflect the increasing importance of industrial products and interest in the beauty of machinery during this period.

Building features include:
- Simple decoration, usually geometric, stylised plant forms, or Maori motifs
- Consistent skyline (one or two storeys, roofs not visible from the street, parapet may be stepped)
- Windows often in pairs or groups of three
- Horizontal proportions emphasised by verandas, bands of decoration, low height, shop front design

Shop fronts:
- Slender frames (bronze or timber)
- Horizontal band of leadlight above door height
- Glazing does not extend to footpath...."

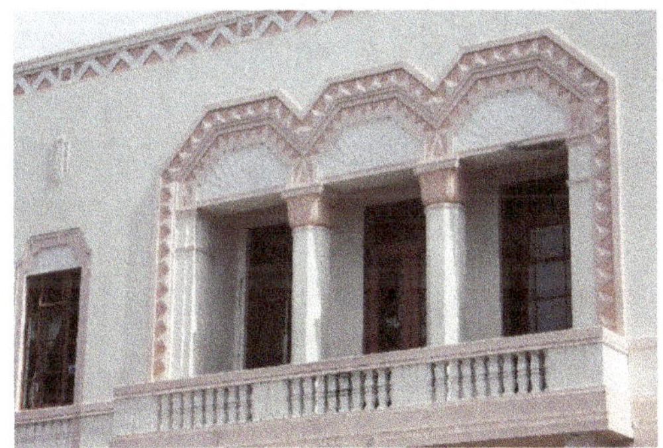

Windows of the former Hotel Central are decorated with geometric, "ziggurat" and sunburst shapes [78]

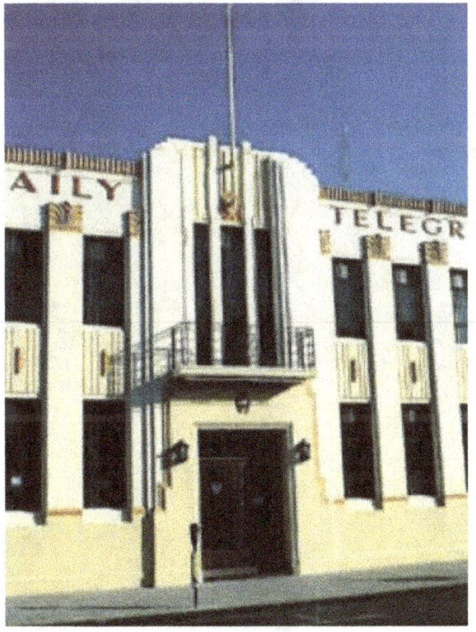

The entrance to the Daily Telegraph building features "ziggurat" forms.

These architectural features derive from ancient Mesotopamia. The Sumerians built large staircases of mud-brick, shaped like a stepped pyramid, which they called **ziggurats**.

---

[77] Art Deco Inventory. Second Edition published 2004. Compiled by Napier City Council with the assistance of the late Robert McGregor who was the Executive Director of the Art Deco Trust. The description of the architectural styles seen in Napier used in the Art Deco Inventory document were extracted from the book, "The Art Deco City" (pub. Art Deco Trust 1998)

[78] Photo by Russell James Smith. 2010. Creative Commons Attribution 2.0 Generic Licence.

1. Stripped Classical Style

The late Robert McGregor[79] outlined "…During the inter-war period, and particularly in the 1920s, classicism as promoted by the École des Beaux Arts in Paris maintained its popularity but in a stripped-down version. Classical details were reduced in number and became 'more-bland', and deep set classical facades with a row of columns beneath a pediment were replaced by engaged columns or shallow pilasters."

He draws our attention to a comparison between the Public Trust building of 1922, the former State Fire Insurance building of 1932-34 (*Devon House at 58 Tennyson Street – designed by Gummer and Ford*), and the T&G building of 1936 that shows the progression from "initially deep to low relief ornamentation" and over time the reduction of the use of these features.

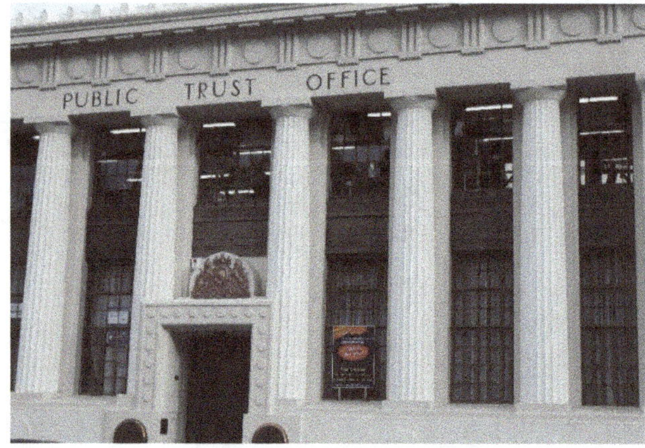

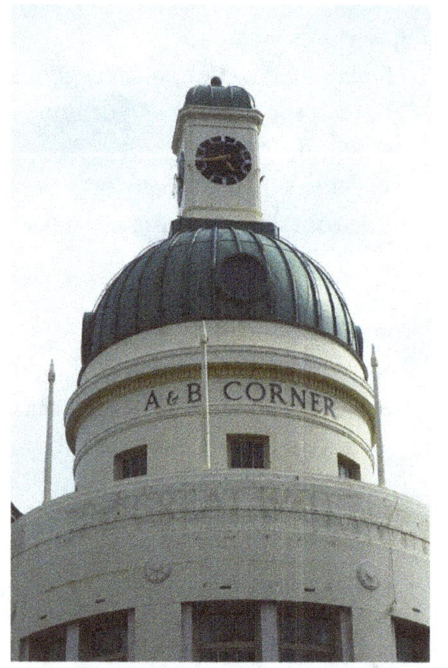

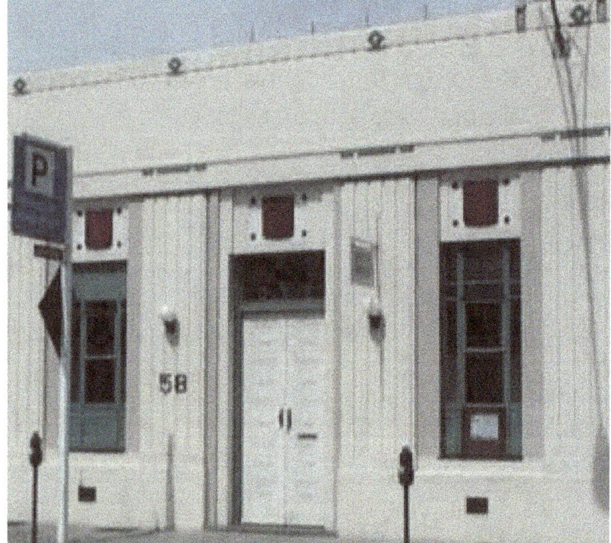

---

[79] Art Deco Inventory. Second Edition published 2004. Compiled by Napier City Council with the assistance of The Art Deco Trust.

The Pioneer Insurance building also utilises these features.

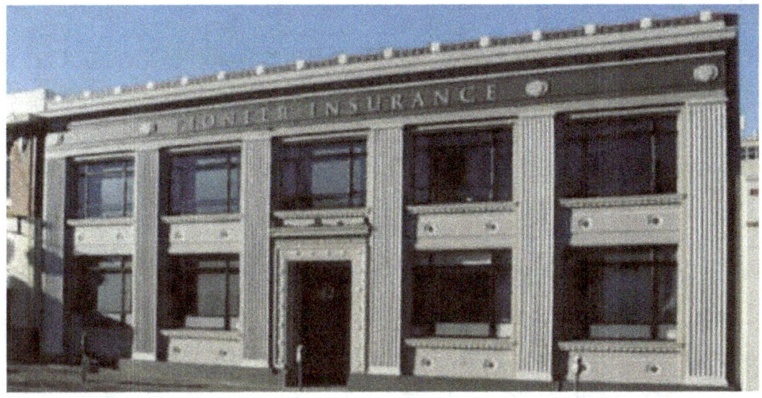

The Stripped Classical style may also incorporate indigenous, modern or even Art Deco ornamental features.

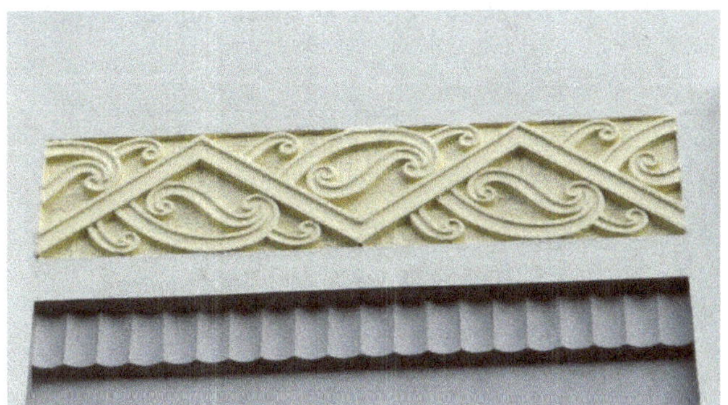

Maori motifs above a window on the ASB Bank building.[80]

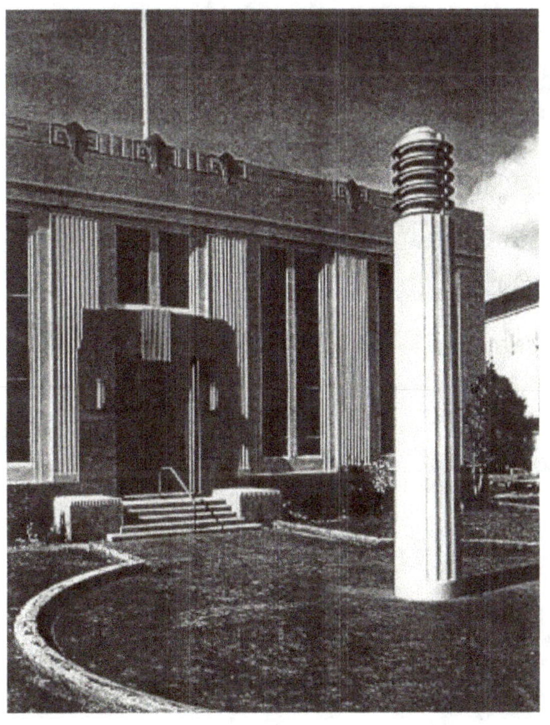

The old Ministry of Works building at 21-23 Browning Street, was designed by the Government architect JT Mair, and completed in 1938 (photo from the Art Deco Inventory).

---

[80] Photo by Jane Nearing from Richardson, US. CC by 2.0 Commons Wikipedia

2. The International Style/Modern(e) Movement

At the Bauhaus Design School (founded in Germany in 1919) the philosophy of "the building as a machine" was adopted. The philosophy was that "form should follow function and an object designed to do its job well must automatically be beautiful." The reason for the name "International Style" was that the style was used world-wide without consideration of local techniques, materials, climate or culture [*McGregor, Art Deco Trust*].

It was also termed the 'Modern or Moderne' movement, and it was the main architectural influence from the 1940s until the 1970s. The features of the buildings include relatively large areas of glazing, use of beam and column construction, and the design did not use applied decorative features relying more on the style and effect of the building itself.

Examples of this style are highlighted as the former AA Building in Herschell Street, the 1954 wing of the Hawke's Bay Museum on the corner of Herschell and Browning Streets, and the former Nurse's Home, on the corner of Spencer Road and Napier Terrace. The architect for all these buildings was Lawrence Williams.

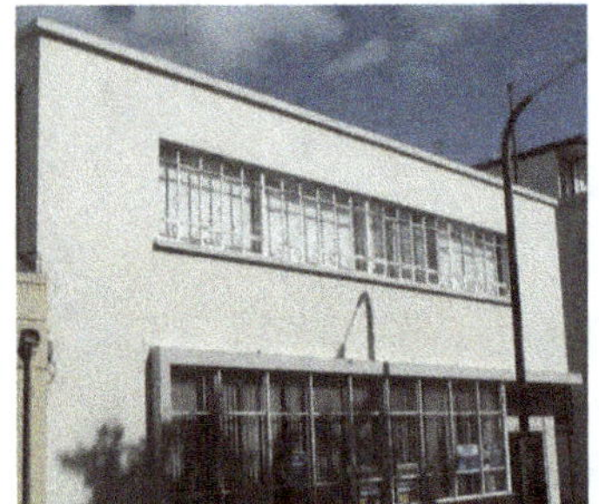
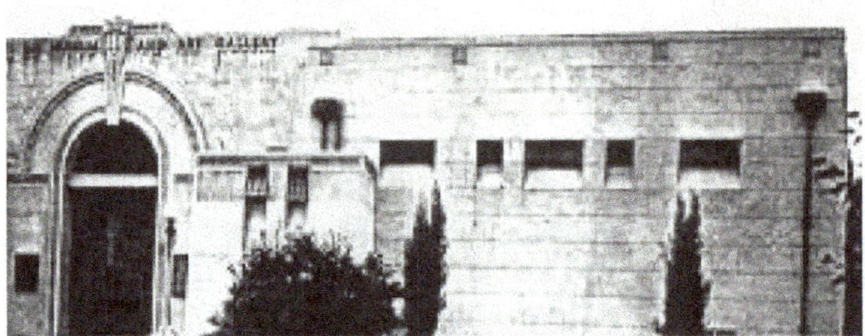

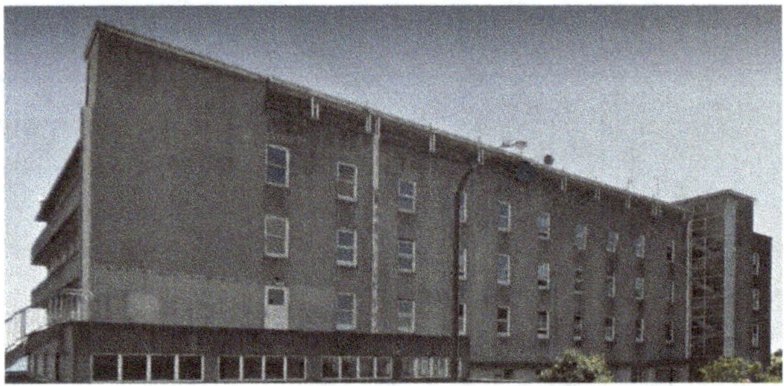

The former NZ Shipping Company building *(left)* on the corner of Byron and Browning Streets and the old Red Cross building *(right)* are other examples of this style:

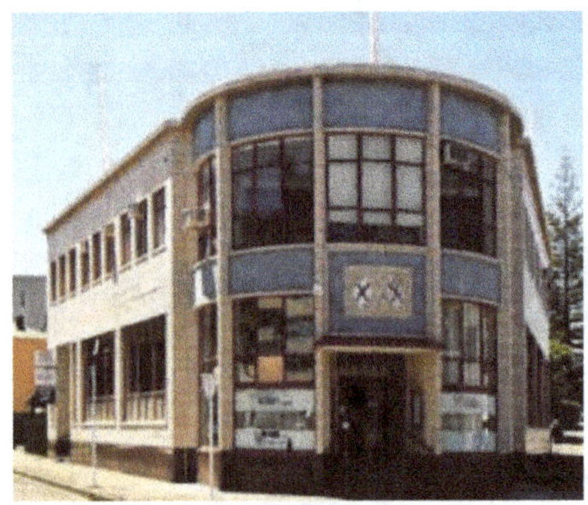
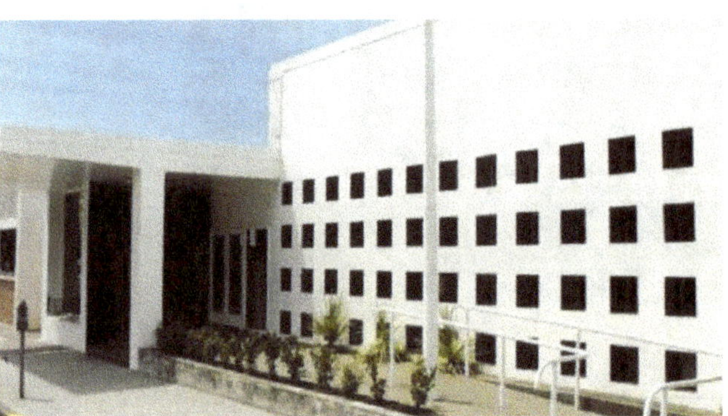

3. Spanish Mission Style

This style originated in the south-west states of North America.

"The Spanish Mission style was popular in new world countries, especially those with climates similar to California. It arrived in New Zealand in 1913 when the Auckland Grammar School was completed, and in Hawke's Bay with Iona College in 1914 and the Hastings Municipal Theatre in 1915, though the former may perhaps be considered more Italian in flavour than Spanish." [*McGregor, Art Deco Trust*]

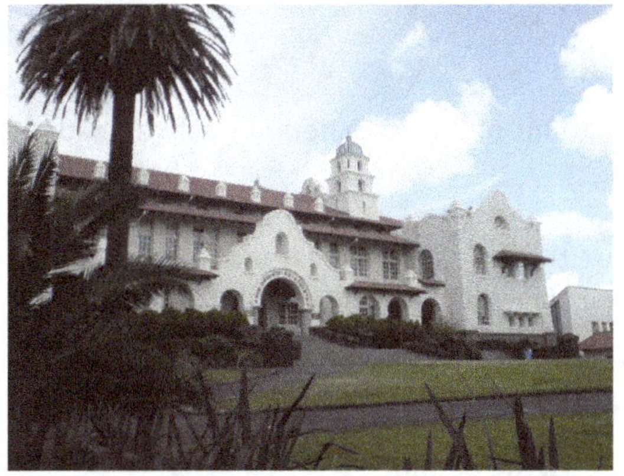

Auckland Grammar School

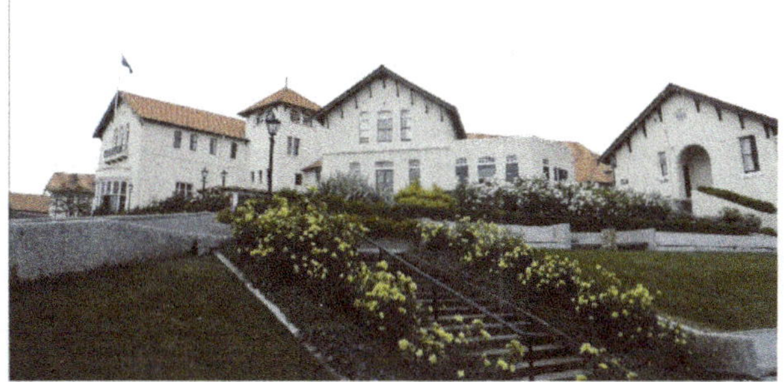

Iona College, Havelock North

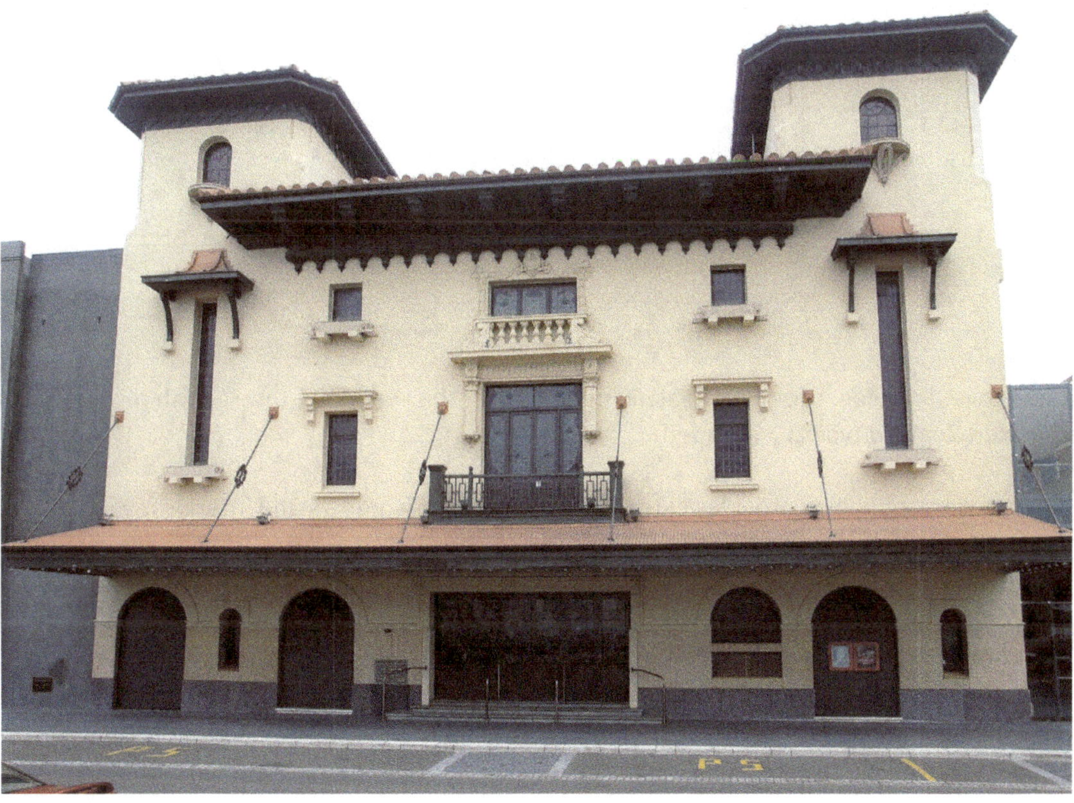

Photo Hastings Municipal Theatre. [81]

---

[81] Photo by Ulrich Lange. Germany. Wikimedia Commons, CC Licence by SA-3.0.

The Spanish Mission style had been adopted in the rebuilding of Santa Barbara, California after an earthquake in 1925, and developed from the simple adobe buildings of the early missions.

The Napier Council signage guidelines outline the typical features:

- Walls are flat with a smooth or textured plaster finish, sometimes relieved with barley twist columns or plaster detailing.
- Terracotta tiles are common on parapets and window hoods.
- Building features include:
    - Terracotta tiled roof/parapet/window hoods
    - Barley twist columns and flat pilasters
    - Balconies or galleries at first floor
    - Windows relatively tall and narrow, or in groups of three, sometimes with arched heads.

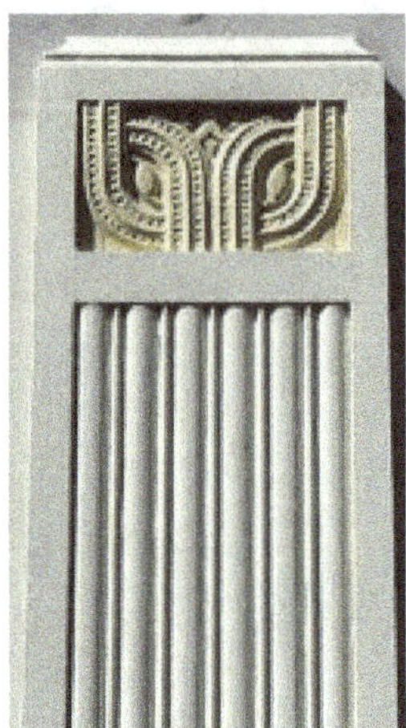

A **pilaster** is an architectural feature that gives the appearance of a supporting column and to delineate a part of a wall, yet it is only ornamental not structural.

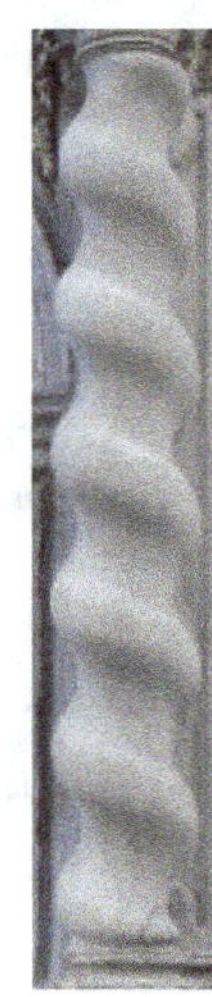

Photo of a Barley Twist column.

The BRANZ renovation guide [82] for New Zealand outlines that the version of the Spanish mission style used in New Zealand typically included:

- poured concrete (which provides extra depth for setback windows and interior reveals)
- a heavier texture to stucco (compared to the art deco style) to more 'authentically' replicate the adobe
- half-round drain pipes to replace the Spanish tiles
- a flat or low-pitched roof clad with corrugated iron
- tall narrow windows with arched heads that were sometimes flanked by timber shutters
- false timber beams protruding from the wall at roof level
- a walled garden to replace the internal courtyard.

---

[82] © **BRANZ** is an independent and impartial research, testing, consulting and information company providing services and resources for the building industry. www.renovate.org.nz/art-deco/siting-layout-and-form/other-1930s-building-styles/

Highlighted examples in Napier include the Criterion Hotel[83], the Provincial Hotel, the Harston's building (see page 53) and the former State Theatre[84].

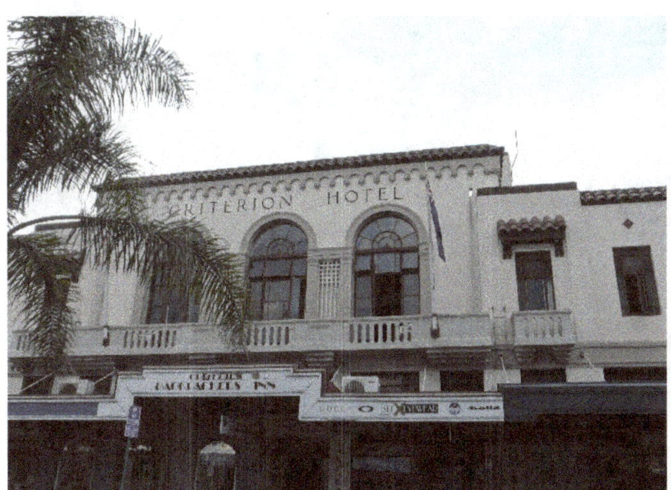

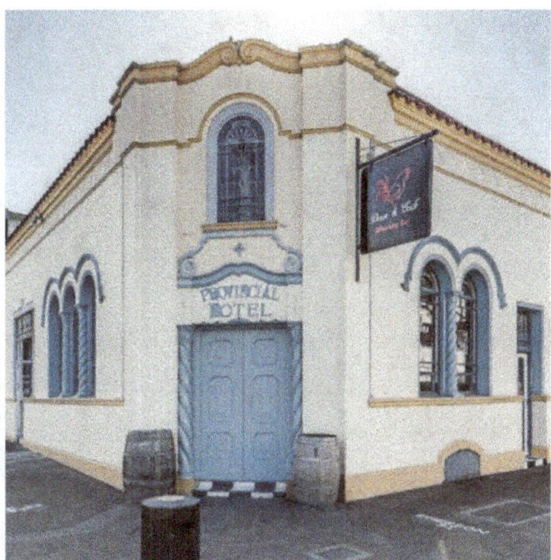

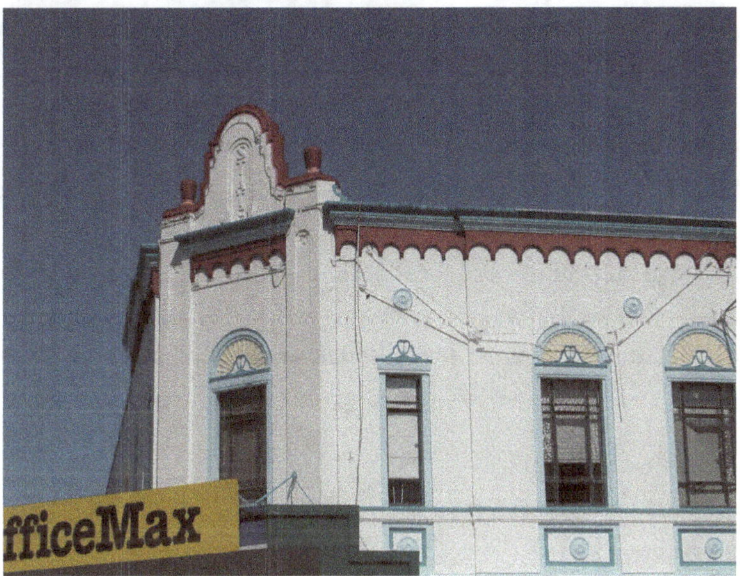

4. The Chicago School and the Prairie Style

The Art Deco Inventory outlines "…The classification of buildings in the Chicago School and the Prairie style often overlaps, since features of the first, which is most associated with Louis Sullivan's work in the 1880s and 1890s, were often seen in early examples of the second. In Napier, courtesy of Louis Hay, the Chicago School can be seen at its best in the Rothmans Building, which uses Sullivan's favourite wide, round 'arch in a cube' form. The old AMP Building has Sullivanesque Art Nouveau ornamentation combined with the smaller round arches which are typical of early Frank Lloyd Wright buildings, designed soon after he left Sullivan's office where he worked and studied."[*McGregor, Art Deco Trust*]

---

[83] Photo by Jane Nearing from Richardson, US. P1220194 [CC BY 2.0 via Wikimedia Commons
[84] Photo by Rich Osborne from UK (NZ2DSCN0037) [CC BY-SA 2.0 (http://creativecommons.org/licenses/by-sa/2.0)], via Wikimedia Commons

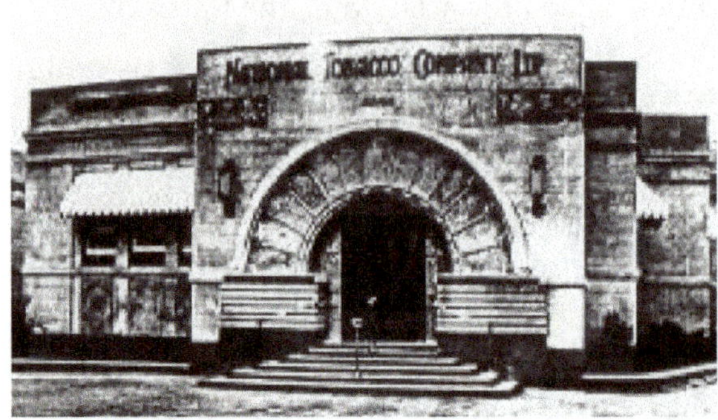
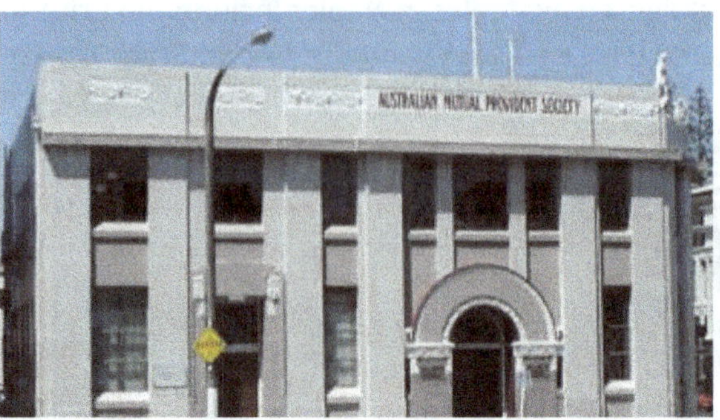

Wright's Prairie houses are typified by the Community Centre in Clive Square (photo left below) and in the restaurant at the north end of the Marine Parade which was built in 1916 (the Former Soldiers' Club).

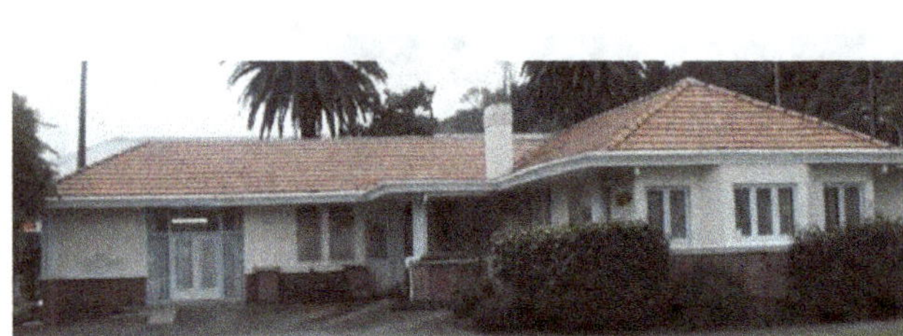
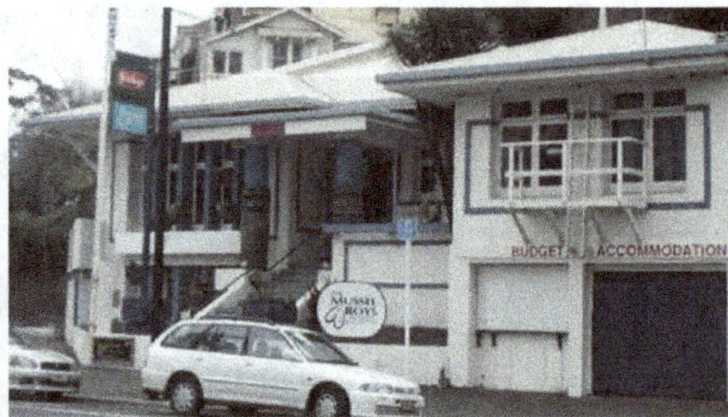

The Napier Council signage guidelines document outlines many of the typical features incorporated in buildings in Napier. It explains that pilasters and fins give the facades a more vertical emphasis and texture is achieved by the use of different materials and incised patterns on the plaster surfaces. Building features include:

- Semi-circular arched doorways
- Windows recessed between columns
- Often no verandah
- Emphasis added to the entrance, by recessing the door between pilasters

Commercial buildings, in addition to the Rothmans and AMP buildings mentioned above, include the old Fire Station (see page 25) and the Hay building (the architect's own building).

Art deco decorative features on a sample of Napier buildings

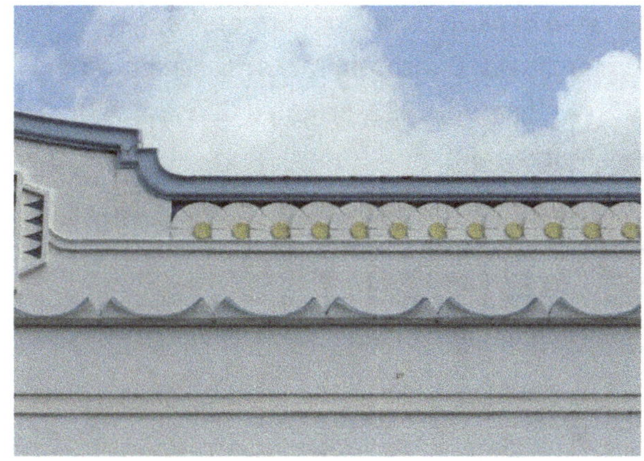

Former Triggs & Morgan building at 131 Emerson Street, also known as the Eastern & Central Trustee Bank Building. Architect: Finch & Westerholm, 1932[85]

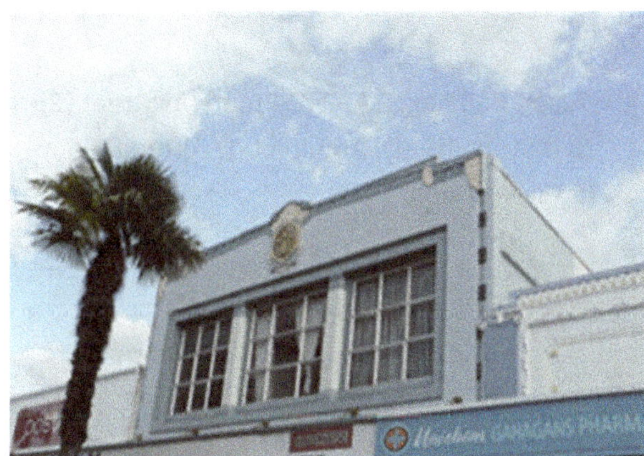

Hurst's Building, 125 Emerson Street Architect: Finch & Westerholm, 1932, Art Deco[86]

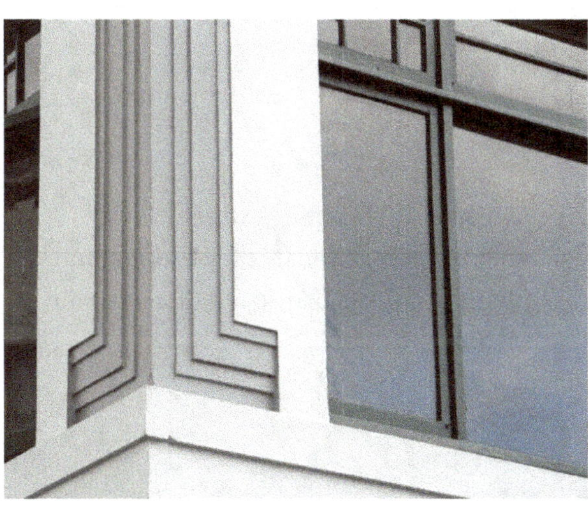

Masonic Hotel, at 64-74 Hastings Street and 2 Tennyson Street. Architects: Prouse & Wilson (designed by Normal Wilson), 1932[87]

---

[85] Photo by Jane Nearing from Richardson, US. CC by 2.0 Commons Wikipedia
[86] Ibid
[87] Ibid

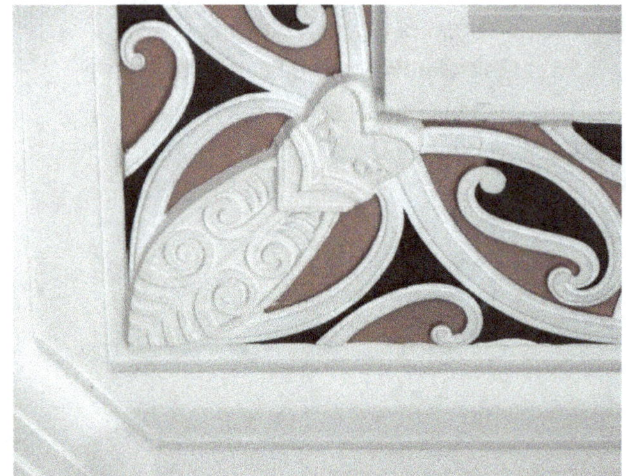

ASB Bank, 100 Hastings Street, Napier. Architect: Chrichton, McKay & Haughton (Wellington) 1932, Stripped Classical with Maori motifs.[88]

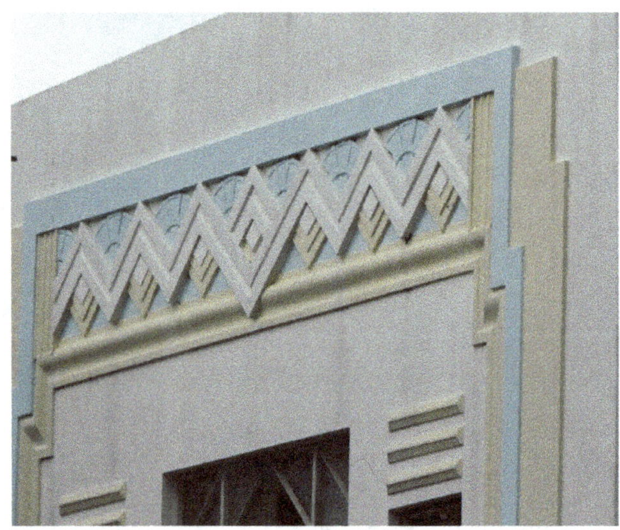

Kidson Building, 170-172 Emerson Street (26-28 Dalton Street). Architect: H Alfred Hill 1933, Art Deco. [89]

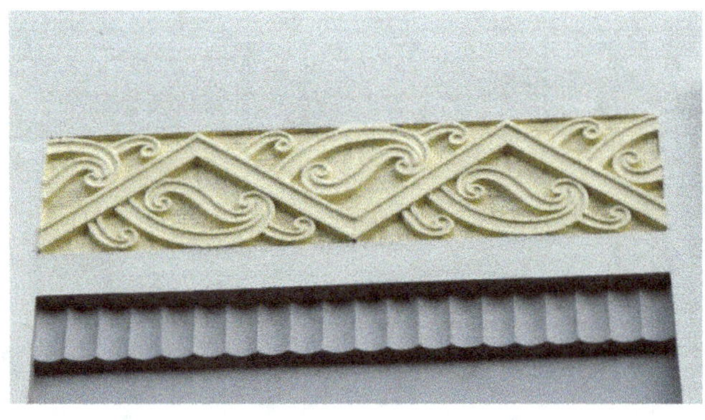

ASB Bank, 100 Hastings Street, Napier. Architect: Chrichton, McKay & Haughton (Wellington) 1932, Stripped Classical with Maori motifs. [90]

---

[88] Photo by Jane Nearing from Richardson, US. CC by 2.0 Commons Wikipedia
[89] Ibid.
[90] Ibid.

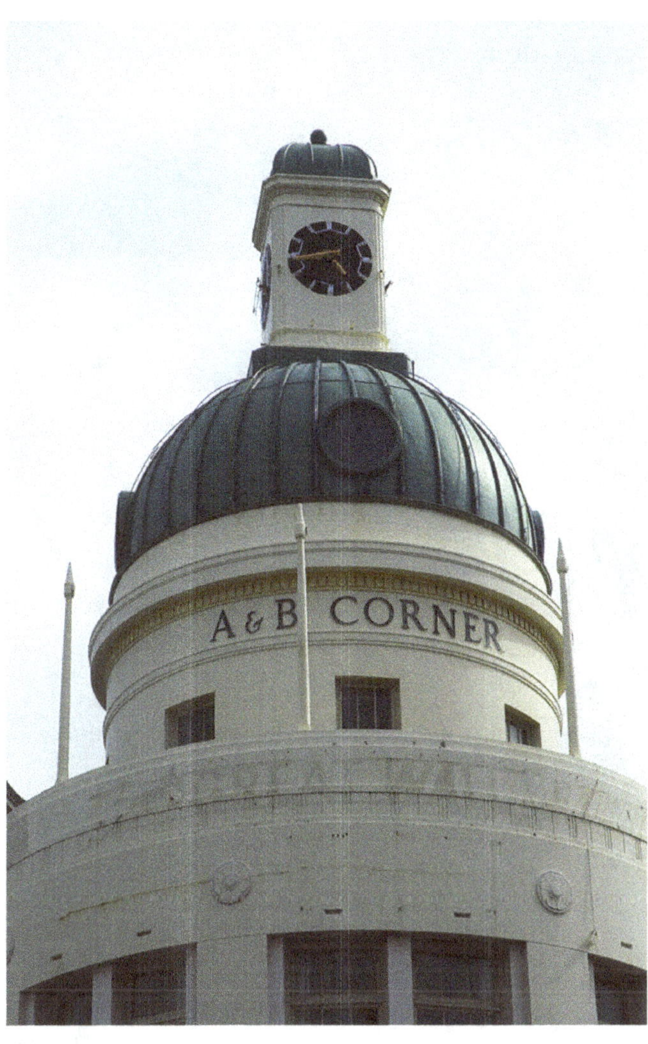

The cupola of the T & G Building, 1 Emerson Street. Architect: Atkin & Mitchell, Wellington, in 1936. Stripped Classical. [91]

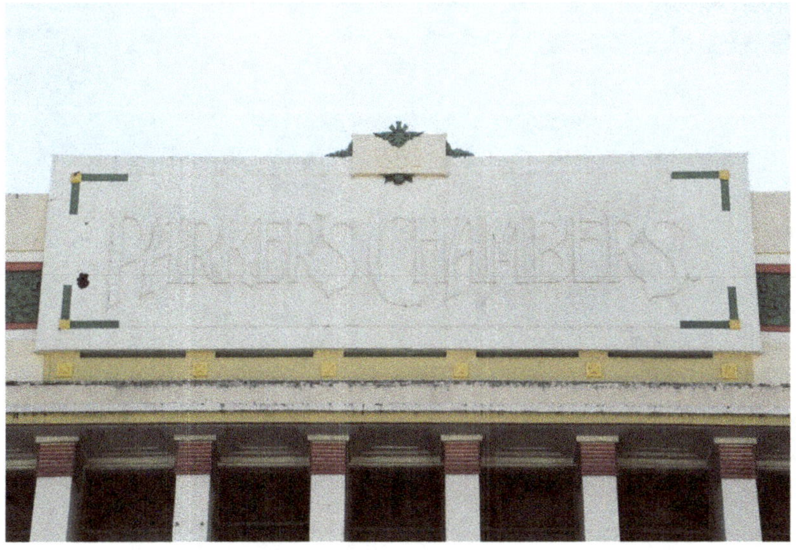

Parker's Chambers at 10 Herschell St and 25a Hastings Street. The 1929 original building was at the Herschell street end, and in 1931-32 the new building was reconstructed at the Hastings Street end. [92]

---

[91] Photographer: James Shook, 26 January 2005. CC by 2.5 Commons Wikipedia

[92] Photo by Geoff Wilson from Christchurch, New Zealand. CC by Share Alike 2.0 Generic

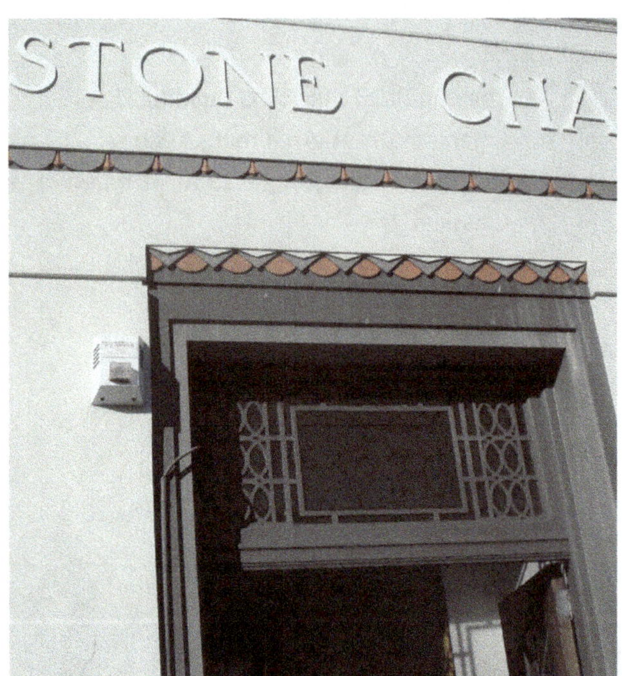

Gladstone Chambers, 50 Tennyson Street. Architect: Finch & Westerholm, 1932. Art Deco. [93]

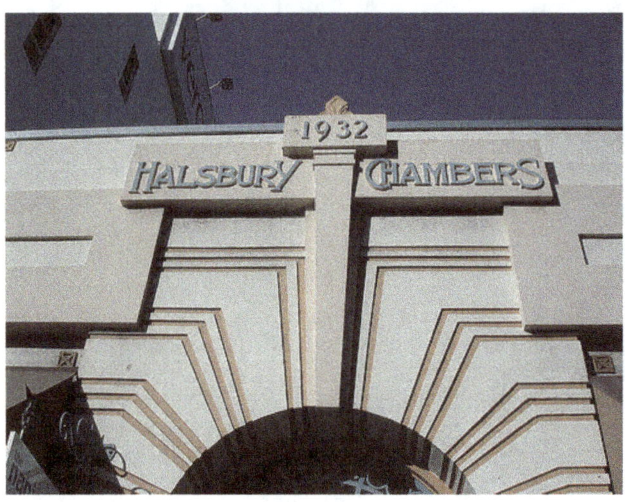

Halsbury Chambers, 74 Tennyson Street. Architect: JA Louis Hay, 1932. Stripped Classical.[94]

The iconic Soundshell on the Marine Parade, with the colonnaded surrounds, was built in 1935 following the 1931 earthquake. It was designed by Napier architect J T Watson, and was a project undertaken and funded by the Thirty Thousand Club.[95]

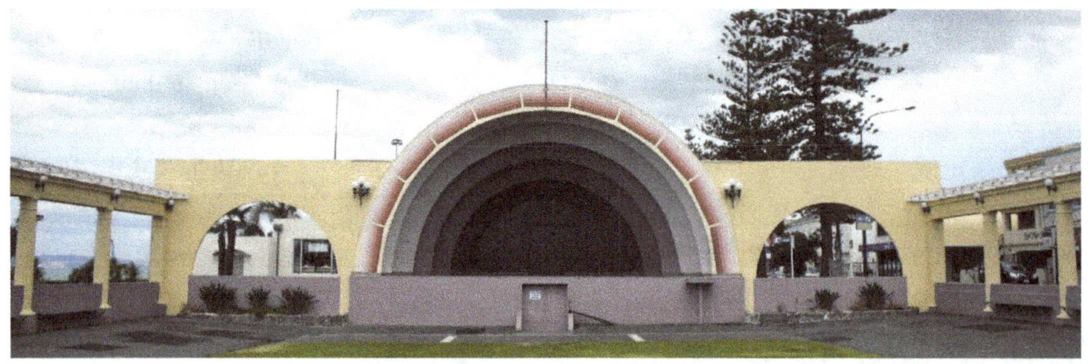

---

[93] Photo by Teacher Traveler. Creative Commons Attribution-Share Alike 2.0 Generic

[94] Ibid.

[95] Photo by Russell James Smith, 2010; cropped for inclusion. Flikr - Creative Commons Attribution 2.0 Generic licence (CC by 2.0)

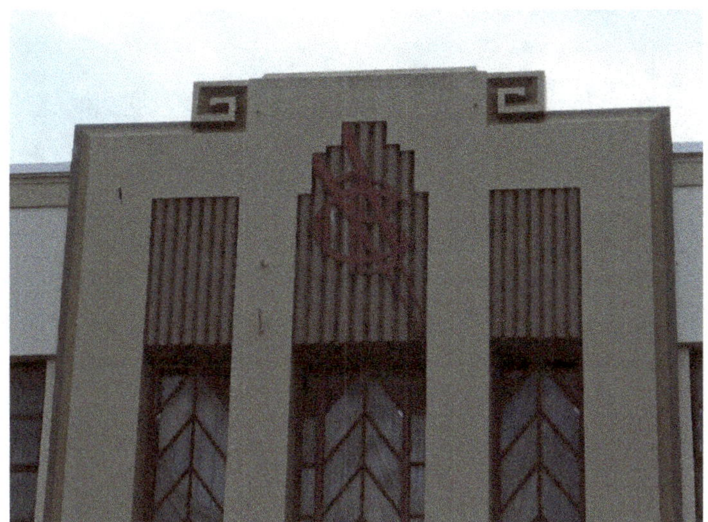

HB Chambers, 78-82 Emerson Street. Architect: EA Williams. 1932, Art Deco.[96]

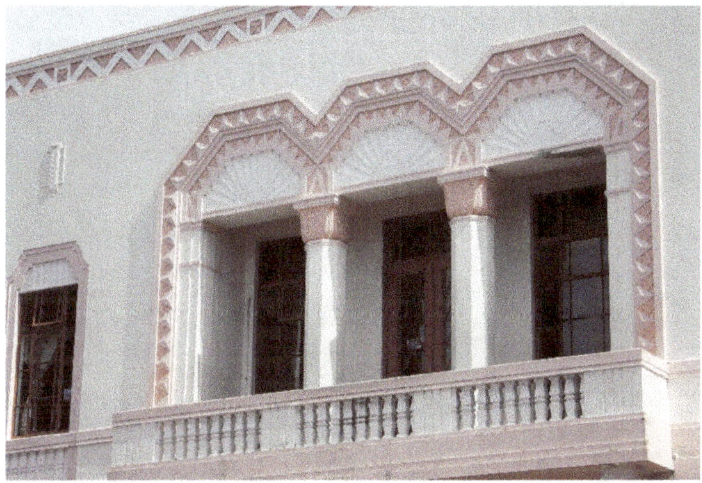

Central Hotel, 47-61 Dalton Street and 183-187 Emerson Street. Architect: EA Williams (Napier) 1932. Style: Art Deco. [97]

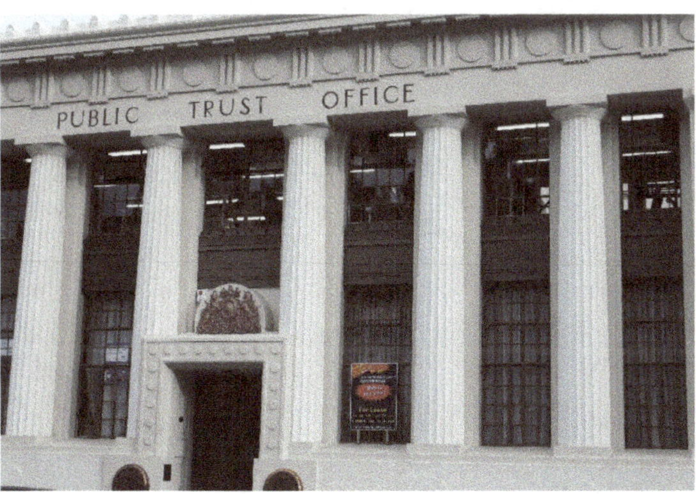

The Public Trust Office building at 100 Tennyson Street was built in 1921 and repaired and strengthened in 1931. The architects were Hyland & Phillips in 1921 and Stanley W Fearn of Wellington in 1931. Its style is described as "classical revival" [98]

---

[96] Photo by Jane Nearing from Richardson, US. CC by 2.0 Commons Wikipedia

[97] Photo by Russell James Smith. 2010. Creative Commons Attribution 2.0 Generic Licence.

[98] Photo by Anne Beaumont, Creative Commons Attribution-Share Alike 2.0 Generic licence, Commons Wikimedia